SPEAKEASY

SPEAKEASY

CLASSIC COCKTAILS REIMAGINED, FROM NEW YORK'S EMPLOYEES ONLY BAR

Jason Kosmas & Dushan Zaric

Foreword by Dale DeGroff

Afterword by David Wondrich

PHOTOGRAPHY BY JOHN KERNICK

TEN SPEED PRESS
Berkeley

Published in the United States by Ten Speed Press,
an imprint of the Crown Publishing Group,
a division of Random House, Inc., New York.

www.crownpublishing.com

www.tenspeed.com

Ten Speed Press and the Ten Speed Press colophon are
registered trademarks of Random House, Inc.

Library of Congress Cataloging-in-Publication Data

Kosmas, Jason.

  Speakeasy : classic cocktails reimagined, from
New York's Employees Only bar /Jason Kosmas and
Dushan Zaric ; photography by John Kernick.

       p. cm.

  Includes index.

  Summary: "A drinks cookbook from the mixologist
owners of Employees Only, a speakeasy-themed bar/
restaurant in New York, with 85 recipes for modern
cocktails inspired by classic drinks"—Provided by
publisher.

  1. Cocktails. I. Zaric, Dushan. II. Kernick, John.
III. Employees Only (Bar) IV. Title.

 TX951.K66 2010

 641.8'74—dc22

                                          2010016567

ISBN 978-1-58008-253-2

Printed in Singapore

Design by Toni Tajima

10 9 8 7 6 5 4 3 2 1

First Edition

NOTE: Some of the recipes in this book include raw eggs. When eggs are consumed raw, there is always the risk that bacteria, which is killed by proper cooking, may be present. For this reason, always buy certified salmonella-free eggs from a reliable grocer, storing them in the refrigerator until they are served. Because of the health risks associated with the consumption of bacteria that can be present in raw eggs, they should not be consumed by pregnant women, the elderly, or any persons who may be immuno-compromised. The author and publisher expressly disclaim responsibility for any adverse effects that may result from the use or application of the recipes and information contained in the book.

Contents

Foreword

I MET JASON KOSMAS AND DUSHAN ZARIC at what may be one of Keith McNally's most popular bars, Pravda, where I was a consultant. Some people in the hospitality business just "get it," and from the beginning these two were naturals. Jay and Dushan embraced the cocktail culture that Keith and I were pursuing as a core theme for Pravda. They understood that it was much more than just a drink—it was a complete experience, a return to classic recipes made with real ingredients and craft bartending techniques—but also a return to a service style from another era.

Both Jay and Dushan went on to manage the bar staff and just after the new millennium decided that the time was right for a different sort of speakeasy, and so they opened Employees Only. This speakeasy, unlike the ones run by gangsters where a good drink was rare and bad ones cost a fortune, celebrated premium products and classic bar service *and* you could walk right into the joint . . . no password necessary.

Employees Only captured the hearts of New Yorkers and the joint has been full since the doors opened. The timing was impeccable—New York was ready for a late night place with solid food and great drinks. Ten years later and again the timing is impeccable; the book *Speakeasy* will hit the shelves at the most exciting time in the history of the American cocktail. *Speakeasy* gives the reader an inside look at the creative process brought to bear in crafting the retooled classic cocktails. The reader can share in the creative process more fully by producing their own homemade syrups, cordials, and infusions.

New York has always been the home of great bar culture—it may be our most important natural resource. I say natural because after two hundred years the bar and grill seems as natural to New York City as the redwoods do to California. Employees Only, along with other pioneering bars like Milk & Honey and Pegu Club, has created a new template for the New York bar that is inspiring imitators both here and abroad. Jay and Dushan are returning to the classics and reinventing the classics, but most importantly they are in the vanguard to return bartending to a craft profession again.

—Dale DeGroff

Acknowledgments

THIS BOOK COULD NOT HAVE HAPPENED were it not for a small army of dear people who have helped either during development, with inspiration and mentoring, or just simply by giving support during the last twelve years since we first started toying with the idea of writing down our recipes and techniques. So all of you listed below—please accept our most sincere gratitude for everything you have done to make this book happen.

First and foremost we would like to thank our wives, Carolyn Kosmas and Jelena Zaric, for their unselfish support, patience, and the courage to stick it out with the two of us and our nightlife careers. Our daughters—Lola, Mia, and Uma—for inspiration and the opportunity to serve for a smile as a tip. We would also like to thank our partners from Employees Only—Igor Hadzismajlovic, Billy Gilroy, and Henry LaFargue—for their support, love, wisdom, and hard work, without which we would never be able to have such an amazing restaurant.

Our chef, Julia Jaksic, and sous chef, Josh Blakely, who so selflessly shared their kitchen with us and let us intrude into their space whenever we had even the dumbest of ideas.

Our Employees Only bar staff, current and past, the boys with tattoos who simply rock! You guys are the baddest, meanest, and most soulful gang in the world. We salute and thank you. Our bar manager, Robert Krueger, who is the smartest student we ever had and a man who has in time become a master in his own right. This book was majorly helped by a last minute save from master barmen Dev Johnson and Bratislav Glisic.

Employees Only's general manager, Stephanie Markowitz, who provided us with guidance, clarity of thought, and lots of love. All the EO managers, servers, bussers, food runners, door people, kitchen people, coat check girls, porters, and psychic ladies who stood in the trenches with us all these years. Rebecca Kahikina, our office manager, for all the hard and sometimes unnecessary work that we load onto her.

All our customers, guests, regulars, and fans—thank you for your support and loyalty. Employees Only exists because of you.

We cannot forget to thank our literary agent Donna Bagdasarian for her love and faith in us and especially for her patience. Honey—

we are sorry for all the drama we gave you; you know we love you.

All the great people at Ten Speed Press, in particular Lisa Westmoreland, for their foresight and courage to sign us up; and especially our editors, Dawn Yanagihara and Sara Golski; and creative director, Nancy Austin, and art director Toni Tajima, for making sure that in reality we have a great book. Our photographer, John Kernick, whose photos blew our socks away and made us, our restaurant, and our drinks look really damn good.

Personally, we also wish to thank our mentor, teacher, and friend Dale DeGroff for all the teachings and inspiration. Dale, you gave us our careers, taught us, inspired us, and always lead by example to show what a real professional bartender should be.

Our friend Simon Ford from Plymouth Gin who supported us and always had our back.

Thank you, Mr. Gilbert John Barretto, for all the wisdom, guidance, and help to make us more balanced individuals and men who understand that a life lived is a life of service.

We also wish to thank Keith McNally and Anna Opitz for all the experience we learned while working for them at Pravda in SoHo.

Our dear friends from Jean Georges Culinary Concepts, Frank Soto and James Gersten, who gave us the opportunity to teach and give back.

Our cocktail-nerd community deserves a huge thank-you as well for the amazing effort of making the American cocktail a part of the mainstream today. Most notably we would like to thank Dave Wondrich, Gary Regan, Tony Abou-Ganim, Audrey Saunders, Julie Reiner, James Meehan, Eben Freeman, Aisha Sharpe, Willy Shine, Ann Tuennerman, Steve Olson, Paul Pacult, Sasha Petraske, Eben Klemm, Jacques Bedenzenhuit, Julio Bermejo, Thomas Estes, Marcovaldo Dionysos, Scott Beattie, H. Joseph Ehrmann, Eric Seed, Phil Ward, and all the rest whose names are now escaping us but you know we are thinking of you as well.

Finally, we wish to thank the countless unknown American bartenders who have passed on the teachings of the bartending trade down through the centuries to us. Thank you for giving us the chance to now be the last link in the chain and to have earned the right to pass it on. We hope we have made you proud.

—Jason Kosmas and Dushan Zaric

Introduction

IN LATE 2001, a small group of bartenders at the most popular bars in downtown Manhattan saw the writing on the wall: chefs in the vanguard were beginning to use ingredients that they touted on their menus as "homemade," "handcrafted," and "organic," and the public was paying attention. The bartenders saw change coming to their craft, too. The days of the vodka Martini were numbered. So they launched a project to change the way people were drinking in their town. Little did they know that they would help destroy bottle service, bring back classic cocktail culture, and singlehandedly revive the mustache.

PAVING THE WAY FOR CLASSIC COCKTAILS

Our story begins in 1998, when we were young, eager bartenders behind the wildly fashionable bar Pravda, located in Manhattan's über-hip SoHo neighborhood. Pravda, a Soviet Russia–themed subterranean vodka and Martini bar, was envisioned by restaurant mogul Keith McNally and opened in 1996 under the tutelage of Dale DeGroff, the most influential figure in the rebirth of the cocktail. Pravda was one of

the first bars to take the leap into making drinks with fresh juices and Boston shakers. Ironically, the classic American bar style was the heart of the communist-themed lounge. Pravda's cocktail menu was heavy on vodka, with more than nine homemade infusions on the menu and more than a hundred frozen vodkas from all over the world. But the cocktails incorporated fresh and seasonal ingredients and were executed in the classic style of bartending, focusing on technique and balance of flavor. Any drink on the menu made with vodka served up could be called a Martini. This opened up enormous possibilities of what could go into a Martini. Pravda set a new level of quality and expertise that few other restaurants could live up to.

Your then-young, fearless authors worked at Pravda, and we quickly became friends. After closing, we would sit in big armchairs and share stories, drinks, ideas, and laughter, unwinding from another frenzied evening of bartending. Before long, we were the major contributors to the direction of Pravda's cocktail menu. The timing coincided with the emergence of a new American interest in good food. The nation was getting its first taste of the Food

Network, and chefs were reaching celebrity status. People became obsessed with writings and publications about food, and the Internet made information accessible to all those who sought it. In the world of mixology, the Martini was the perfect medium to incorporate strange and exotic fruits and herbs not seen before in cocktails. The moniker *Martini* gave consumers a comfort level in ordering these wild new concoctions. The Martini became the gateway drug that eventually pulled people into the world of classic drink making—a vehicle for introducing then-uncommon ingredients such as pomegranates, blood oranges, and kumquats. We crafted our own syrups and revised the existing recipes with all-natural ingredients. The infusions once made with sweetened sulfured dried fruit now contained both fresh and dried organic produce.

After working at Pravda for more than a year, Dale DeGroff held a follow-up training there. Dale is the godfather, the James Brown of drink making. Dale spoke of the history of the cocktail and instilled in us a pride to treat our jobs as a profession. He described it as a centuries-old craft handed down from generation to generation. He gave us an original copy of the *How to Mix Drinks or the Bon Vivant's Companion*—the first-ever cocktail book, published in 1862 by the father of our profession, the "Professor," Jerry Thomas. We had an epiphany as to how many generations had delved into its secrets. It compelled us to research the foundations of cocktail making and resurrect long-lost ideas. As there was no demand for such books at the time, we easily created our own library,

thanks to eBay and used bookstores. We lined up our books chronologically to make comparisons, draw conclusions, and witness the evolution of the cocktail. Dale continued to periodically instruct us over the next few years as we developed our own style.

Crafting homemade ingredients like the masters of old became our focus. Moving beyond one-note cocktails, we raided the kitchen to develop intricate flavors. We began to realize that vodka as a spirit was preventing our cocktails from realizing their full potential. It simply does not contribute any flavor. We reached for gin, brandy, and rye whiskey—and our drinks came bursting to life. However, these cocktails clearly had no place in a vodka Martini bar—and now, neither did we.

CHANGE IN THE CITY

The real push for us to open our own bar came after September 11, 2001. Before that date, New York was an exciting city with an air of perpetual adolescence, and we were reaping the benefits of all this lifestyle had to offer. After the initial shock of the terrorist attacks, the downtown New York restaurant and nightlife scene seemed to change. People contend that America lost its innocence that day, but it also lost its naughtiness. Nightlife in the city became sporadic, sober, and dull. Destinations that used to be open until 4 a.m. were closing their doors early; only a handful of restaurants stayed open past midnight. New York's restaurant employees were the ones most affected by this. Our income became inconsistent, and there were few options to go out to after a hard night's work. While mega-clubs and bottle service dominated the late-night scene, restaurant employees would gather in small dark pubs, sharing stories. There was a sense of camaraderie among us misfits (who, by the way, now run and own some of the best restaurants and bars in the country). We wanted to capture this feeling and bottle it.

Our ambitions were simple: to open up a first-class cocktail bar that would be entirely owner operated. Over the course of a week, we would completely staff that bar ourselves, creating a direct link between the customer and the establishment. We wanted to transport people back to a time when drinking cocktails was part of a lifestyle, and to romanticize it. A secluded destination was ideal for this concept, to keep out the distractions of daily life and reserve the restaurant for people in the know. Many locations we scouted were too big for our original concept, so we envisioned a faux business exposed to the street with two swinging doors passively marked "Employees Only," which would lead into our hidden cocktail den. Employees Only came to represent the fact that we, the owners, were also working there (see our photo on page 8). It also beckoned our intended audience of peers in the business. Finally, it created a barrier between the real world and the restaurant industry.

DRAWING INSPIRATION FROM THE SPEAKEASY

We found the perfect metaphor to romanticize our concept in the speakeasies of the 1920s Prohibition era. It was a time when cocktails were truly forbidden fruit and finding them was a risky, clandestine adventure. To be historically correct, however, we should point out that few speakeasies looked like Francis Ford Coppola's *Cotton Club*. Most were little more than dingy basements with a wood plank on top of two barrels and a couple of chairs. This may sound disenchanting, but speakeasies were also the first places where it was socially acceptable for women to drink with men. Flappers emerged, and, together with fellow male imbibers, took their chances in defying the new law.

Don't think for a moment that, in their defiance, people were raising perfectly crafted cocktails. Most speakeasies served whatever alcohol they could get their hands on. Most drinks that were served were horrible—and some, containing poisonous methyl alcohol, were even lethal. Many of the mixed drinks created during Prohibition fell into one of two categories: those designed to mask the flavor of bad hooch and those created outside of the country. Either way, Prohibition accelerated the evolution of the cocktail and exported it around the world.

Before Prohibition, cocktails were a purely American phenomenon. They represented the melting pot of the inhabitants of this young country. The idea of "bastardizing" a spirit was appalling to most in Europe, where the cocktail did not progress past simple aperitifs. When the reality of Prohibition set in, many well-to-do Americans vacationed in other countries where booze flowed like water. Realizing this, expert bartenders discovered new places to display their craft. Some emigrated to Caribbean islands such as Cuba, a mere ninety miles from U.S.

shores; others fled to Europe and Great Britain, where drinking was part of the daily lifestyle. Cities like London, Paris, and Milan became the stomping grounds of the thirsty American elite.

Out of these migrations, new cocktails were born. Influenced by their surroundings, bartenders in the Caribbean crafted tropical cocktails with new flavors never seen before in mixology. In Europe, many expanded on the aperitif, and old-world flavors crept into cocktail making. New spirits and bitters native to these countries increased the complexity of the cocktails created there. Back in the United States, the small number of speakeasies had to play down the poor quality of bathtub gin, white lightning, and the merchandise of rum runners. Some had to become *very* creative.

Though Prohibition ended up a failed experiment and many of the cocktails consumed in the speakeasies are best forgotten, drinking was changed forever. Mixology was recognized as a culinary art form around the globe, and cocktails as the first original American contribution to the world of gastronomy. By the time Prohibition was repealed on December 5, 1933, cocktails had attained worldwide acceptance and influence. The notion of what could be a cocktail had expanded exponentially. Seventy years later, we decided to take this idea and romanticize it, to give it our own incarnation. We realized that most restaurateurs were bringing Paris and Shanghai to New York, yet no one was trying to preserve what New York was infamous for. Employees Only would be a New York speakeasy.

THE COCKTAILS

The vision behind the bar at Employees Only was to take a culinary approach to classic mixology. All cocktails would be either reenvisioned or modified classics or inspired by classic themes or ingredients. By blending drinks with homemade and contemporary ingredients, we sought to change the way people perceived the old standards and to make cocktail drinking as fun and accessible as it once had been. In a reprint of *How to Mix Drinks or the Bon Vivant's Companion,* we found our bar jackets in a portrait of a bartender wearing a clean white coat similar to a chef's coat. The white coat would let people know that we were serious about our craft and that great effort went into creating our little masterpieces. (Just for the record, in no way were we pretending to be chefs. We are not chefs; we are bartenders. We have the utmost respect for someone who slaves away in a kitchen creating edible art under heat and pressure.) And because the bartender in question wore the same handlebar mustache as our partner, Igor, the picture was complete.

The mustache thing was a coincidence. When we opened, people wrote rave reviews about the "mustachioed" bartenders of Employees Only. What was really scary was when the mustaches began popping up on the other side of the bar.

In late December 2004, Employees Only opened to a select group of friends and industry colleagues. The turnout and the immediate, overwhelming response were shocking. Within a few months, our little secret was out. People from all walks of life and countries passed through the vestibule to taste our libations. Every night at 6:00 p.m., we opened to a bar full of women. We would joke that we would buy a drink for the first man to get a seat at the bar, which would usually happen around 8:00 p.m. Six months later, we held a seminar in London; more than two hundred people attended to find out more about our little gem. Employees Only had become a world-class neighborhood restaurant.

And over the years, EO has become a New York City institution. On any given night of the week, after midnight we have an additional surge of customers: cooks, bartenders, and industry leaders from around the city. We serve more than 130,000 cocktails each year, making EO one of the highest-grossing cocktail bars per square foot. Since our opening, many "speakeasy" cocktail bars have opened up worldwide, bringing that ambience of intimacy and seclusion to other neighborhoods and cities. Popular American culture has become obsessed with period pieces from the last century, and marketing agencies have begun to use vintage packaging and messages to grab consumers' attention. Restaurants everywhere must now educate their bartenders on proper technique, and bar-restaurant hybrids are found in many major U.S. cities. The greatest compliments that we receive are not from the press but from the young women who dance on the bar one night, then bring their families in for dinner the next to show how mature they are.

They say God protects fools and drunks, and God knows we've got both at Employees Only.

SPEAKEASY

FROM PAST TO PRESENT:
Reimagining Classics for a New Sensibility

"I never thought that the music called 'jazz' was ever meant to reach just a small group of people, or become a museum thing locked under glass like all other dead things that were once considered artistic." —MILES DAVIS

EMPLOYEES ONLY was never intended to be simply a shrine to the classic cocktails. For us, it is paramount to express and share all our knowledge and technique through contemporary interpretation. But reimagining cocktails is not simply a gimmick to lure customers through the door. It is an artistic style of reinterpreting an idea and contemporizing it. Yes, many recipes are timeless, but we do not hold onto the conceptions and flavors that do not apply today.

We think recipes should serve as learning tools for new inspirations. The cocktail culture is only as interesting as its diversity—what a boring world it would be if everyone made drinks in exactly the same way! Fortunately, in cocktails, as in life, there is no true authority that makes these judgments for all to live by. As we will illustrate, it is up to you to try, taste, and figure out what works and what does not.

There are many reasons to reinvent the classics: the craft of bartending has evolved, the times demand it, bartenders have been reinventing since the beginning, we love to play with our creativity and imagination, and sometimes we are tired of jazz and just want to rock it out. Bartenders are craftspeople, and we reinvent classics to preserve the craft. We are the next link in a line of professional bartenders who have been passing the knowledge of mixing drinks from bartender to apprentice since the beginning.

Jerry Thomas's 1862 *How to Mix Drinks or the Bon Vivant's Companion* illustrates what it meant to be a professional bartender during his time—when bartenders needed to understand not only how to make cocktails but also how to manufacture many of the ingredients they used. An early edition includes an apothecary appendix on how to prepare tinctures, tonics, syrups, cordials, vermouths, and the rest. Victorian barkeeps did not have liquor stores on every corner, and many ingredients did not travel far or easily. If they needed raspberry cordial, they had to make it themselves. Bartenders in San Francisco, who required vermouths like those from Italy, learned to blend local wine with herbs, spices, and brandies. This art was lost over the last century as the industrialization of food shaped the way we eat and drink, but with the recent interest in all things local, organic, and artisan, the tide is turning.

At Employees Only, we look to recipes not only as a record of the ingredients and methods used but as a time capsule to teach us how ingredients, techniques, and cocktails themselves evolved. Recipes serve solely as guidelines; some ingredients do not even exist anymore, and few retain their original character. It would be impossible to make many of these drinks exactly as they were intended. But we can read into the flavor profile and direction of the cocktail and try to reincarnate it. When you do not have the specific ingredient a recipe calls for—like Amer Picon—you improvise. You substitute or reimagine the ingredient. This is a key step in the style we now practice.

People drink differently today than they did 150 years ago. For that matter, they drink differently than they did 50 years ago. People today have more accessibility to drinks and spirits than ever before. There are new quality ingredients that would have dazzled the masters of old. As keepers of the trade, we can use these ingredients to create new cocktails in the old style.

Portion size has changed. The cocktails of yore are comparable to a big shot today. Because social drinking for women was scorned prior to Prohibition, the female palate had virtually no influence on traditional cocktail making. Also, we now know that men's and women's bodies handle alcohol differently.

There's been another shift: where luxury ruled for the preceding decades, now value and integrity reign without question. People care about the quality of what they are putting into their bodies. There's a new focus on knowing where items come from and the manner in which they were prepared. Thus our culinary approach to classic mixology. Both of us were fortunate to come from families where cooking was a part of the culture and family lineage, so the art of manufacturing our own ingredients is an expression of who we are as people. Using premium raw materials, we craft our creations for the modern sensibility.

The classic recipes offer tremendous insight into the interplay of ingredients and techniques. Our inspiration comes from those techniques, but it does not end there. Reimagining cocktails also allows us to put our stamp on the world; to bring something completely unique from a mere idea into reality. It allows us to say, "We were here." Every experiment doesn't succeed, of course, but sometimes you create something so amazing you fairly burst with pride. But to break the rules, you first must know what they are. To improvise, you first have to know your standards and scales. That's why we've written this book. The recipes that follow provide both the modern classics and the variations we serve at Employees Only. To help you understand how we conceived our drinks, we have provided the recipes from which they originated as well as any others that influenced the cocktails' makeup. We hope that this system will guide you to craft your own cocktails and imagine new libations.

MASTERING THE
PERFECT COCKTAIL

THE SECRET TO MAKING perfect cocktails is
not measured in ounces. It does not require
shaking. It goes beyond mechanics and is far
more important than technique. It is what sep-
arates a bartender from a paint mixer. It is the
human factor. Mixology is more than following
a recipe to exact measurements and following
directions to perfection. Bartenders influence
their cocktails not only in their execution of a
recipe but also in their intention, interaction,
and communication. Cocktail making becomes
art when your understanding of theoretical
knowledge becomes intertwined with your life
experience. It cannot be forced. This does not
happen overnight and it does not come solely
from reading. It comes from doing, from liv-
ing and experiencing. It comes from trying. To
master this, as in everything you do in life, you
must do it well and to the fullest.

FRESH, HIGH-QUALITY INGREDIENTS
Just as in cooking, the proper choice of ingredients will greatly influence the quality of the
final cocktail. Select only high-quality ingredients. This starts with produce. Lemon, lime,
and other juices should be squeezed fresh,

strained free of pulp, and used within the day.
Because they are free of preservatives, they
should be maintained on ice or kept refrigerated. Garnishes should also be cut fresh and
handled carefully.

Explore the ways in which fresh ingredients play along with spirits, cordials, and even
herbs. Remember, all fruits taste best when
they are locally in season and naturally ripe.
As a nation of consumers, we have lost touch
with this, as most fruits are now available year-
round from around the globe. Certified organic
is not a must in all cases but flavor is. You will
notice that produce that has been responsibly
harvested may lack uniformity, size, and color,
but they exude the true nature of the fruit
and its place of origin. Wild fruits tend to be
smaller than their cultivated counterparts but
are packed with flavor. Anyone who has tasted
a tiny fresh wild strawberry can never go back
to its conventionally grown cousins: oversized,
with cottony white, cucumber-tasting interiors.

Steer clear of commercially processed
cocktail components and mixers, such as sour
mix, Margarita mix, and grenadine. Read their
ingredient lists, and you'll see why we shun

them. You can make many of these in your own kitchen, and believe us, they will taste better than anything on the store shelves. More important, you will be proud to serve them. Think about it: would reputable chefs serve canned gravy? Wouldn't they make it from scratch? Artificial products taste artificial. It is not hard to create your own simple syrup and juice your own lemons to make a real Tom Collins. We challenge you to make your own versions of classic mixers, using pure original ingredients. Please refer to "Homemade Syrups, Cordials, Infusions, and Accompaniments," beginning on page 152, for further suggestions.

When conceiving cocktails, remember that the main objective is to showcase the spirit. The greatest expression of a quality spirit is in its pure form. The spirits used in the recipes in this book were chosen specifically for the flavor of the cocktail. Always strive for the highest potential of that cocktail. In restaurants, cost frequently deters bartenders and patrons from putting better spirits in their drinks. House brands, also known as well spirits, are notoriously inferior; Prohibition speakeasies offered better-quality spirits than what some contemporary bars offer their guests. Fortunately, there are many affordable products out there that can be used to make outstanding drinks. But there's little or no marketing behind many of these inexpensive products, so they are little known to the layperson. Share these secrets with your friends and guests, and they will carry them for life. Simply using the most expensive products does not mean that you are making the perfect cocktail. Consider the actual flavor notes, not the price. Eighteen-year-old rye whiskeys are mellowed by wood and will not offer the same (desirable) raw character that a younger one can in a Whiskey Sour. Aged products are cherished for those subtle characteristics that are frequently lost when mixing them into drinks. The same is often true with tequila in Margaritas. Research where and how products are produced before you buy. Hard spirits like gin, rum, brandy, and whiskey are not the only items you should look into. There are many alcoholic cordials and liqueurs made with wholesome ingredients using natural methods. Stay away from anything with a color not found in nature—the artificial flavors and colors are the same ones used in bubble gum.

In the recipes that follow, we often call for specific brands. Although these are important to the consistency of our restaurant offerings, we realize that some brands may be hard to obtain. When you substitute, try to locate brands that have a flavor profile similar to the ones we suggest.

BALANCE OF INGREDIENTS

Understanding how to attain balance is paramount to making great cocktails. Equilibrium is achieved through individual preference and technique. It all comes down to personal taste, literally and figuratively. It's not only the recipe components that affect how a cocktail tastes; the methods used also shape its structure. The key is to think beyond balancing only sweet and sour. A master bartender must be able to command the body, texture, and finish. For us, mixology is the craft of combining spirits and flavors to produce a new and unique experience that cannot be achieved by the spirits alone, creating harmony among flavors, textures, and aromas. At Employees Only, we begin with the age-old methods and proportions of the American bar and expand that repertoire with more culinary distinctions—flavors that accentuate and contrast each other. Every cocktail should have an element that gives it zing and makes it special. Although many cocktails focus on a balance between sweetness and the spirit, this third dimension gives the drink complexity. A Ramos Gin Fizz would be nothing without orange flower water, but this method is difficult to execute. There are three levels of balance to master. First is the balance of sweetness to dryness. This is typically the first stage in any bartender's development. Second, the balance of sweet and dry to the spirit: is the spirit lost, or does it overpower the other components? The final stage in the evolution of balance is creating a counterbalance—a third dimension. This flavor component works within and around the cocktail to create depth. It is the element that makes the cocktail "pop."

Use the recipes here as guidelines—starting points—as you learn for yourself how to balance cocktails. Just as every musician has a personal sound, you as a trained bartender will taste in your own way. Personal taste and preferences will change and evolve as you grow. Taste everything, all the time. Know your fresh juices. Taste them before you begin; citrus juices taste very differently in different seasons. The more you taste, the better you will get at producing wonderful tastes for your guests.

PASSION, KNOWLEDGE, AND WISDOM

These three personal qualities are essential components for making the perfect cocktail. We address passion first because it is often ignored by many in our profession. Many people become bartenders just to make money. There is no love for the work, and for many the job is actually a burden. To others, bartending is the ability to make drinks following a predetermined recipe, measuring every ingredient precisely. Similar to baking, this approach requires measuring devices to make cocktails consistently. It doesn't take into account seasonal ingredients that change week to week and go in and out of season locally. It also doesn't take into account what the person making the drink contributes to the cocktail. To make good cocktails, you have to want to. Our best advice is to practice making drinks for the people you care for. This is why grandma's cooking tastes so good—because it is made with love. Pour your soul and passion into your cocktails, and you will quickly see the difference. No art exists in a vacuum, so bring your creations into the world and let others witness them. Remember, you don't have to be a cocktail snob to be able to mix drinks; you need only the will and passion to do so. If your passion is real, everything else will seem effortless.

When it comes to knowledge, some readers may be at a disadvantage. You may not work in the restaurant industry or have the desire to; you may not have encountered many spirits nor have a working knowledge of cocktail recipes and their histories. That is OK. There are plenty of home enthusiasts who can make a mean Sazerac or a delicately balanced Aviation. Knowledge is something you can acquire. It is, in fact, the only thing that we can pass on to you directly. Keep in mind that we are sharing here not all of our experiences but only those we deem most important. There is much more you can learn from others. There are plenty of great books on the market, and internet research is an easy way to find bits of information and compare what different people are doing. The vintage cocktail books now being reprinted are great resources. Just take everything with a grain of salt. Times have changed, and tastes have changed with them. Just because you know the recipe to the Corpse Reviver No. 2 and all its versions printed in the Savoy cocktail book does not mean that you can make good cocktails.

Many people believe that bartending schools are the quick and easy answer. Unfortunately, these offer little more than what you could achieve on your own with books. Most use colored water and flashcards in a vain attempt to teach you the art. This is no different than a culinary school teaching cooking with a rubber chicken and a cookbook. Anyone can memorize recipes and measure a perfect shot. It takes a trained palate to properly learn the craft of mixology. Find out for yourself what is out there and how people are doing it. As is the case with all knowledge, to make it yours you must put it into practice.

Wisdom is gained by doing, and in mixology, you must learn the craft before you can hone it. It is no easier to master than carpentry or metallurgy. It is through repetition that we see not only how but also why we do things. Make the same cocktail over and over and taste each to see how subtle changes affect flavor. Taste a variety of cocktails from different bartenders. Examine not only what goes into a recipe but how the ingredients work together. See how a recipe is affected by trying variations on an ingredient. Try different proportions. As in many crafts, we learn partly from example or apprenticing. Many bars train their barbacks to provide everything a bartender needs so bartenders can focus on servicing the customers; however, those who are eager to become bartenders use their time behind the bar to learn from their mentors. The young bartender learns as much from mistakes as from successes.

TOOLS AND TECHNIQUES

Like every craftsperson, you'll need to acquire the right tools and learn how to use them. The following is a concise list of the tools and techniques applicable to how we create our cocktails at Employees Only. In addition to the bar tools, we have listed many common kitchen utensils standard to home cooking. We do not use any molecular techniques or advanced chemistry beyond a hard shake, so no specialized equipment is needed. We first present the tools in the order of frequency of use. Techniques follow in a similar manner, beginning with the most basic methods in drink making.

Pour Spouts

Pour spouts make free pouring of liquor clean and accurate. Made of either metal or plastic, they mount easily in the opening of most bottles, fastened by a small plastic ribbed grommet that creates a tight seal within the rim. Over time, however, the grommet's shape may become worn from overuse. To reconstitute it, place it in warm water for a few minutes, then shock it in an ice-cold bath; the plastic will return to its original shape.

16-Ounce Mixing Glass

The 16-ounce mixing glass is the most important tool, as nearly all cocktails are built in it. It is part of the Boston shaker (see below) and is also used on its own for stirred cocktails in combination with the julep strainer (see right). The mixing glass is necessary for free pouring of cocktails, as it is transparent and will help you see exactly how much liquid is going in without the aid of a measuring device.

Boston Shaker

The Boston shaker is a 24-ounce metal tumbler used like a lid with the 16-ounce mixing glass to make shaken cocktails. The metal shaker fits around the rim of the mixing glass to form an airtight seal. It is important that the metal shaker be strong enough to hold a seal but malleable enough to expand on and off the glass.

Hawthorn Strainer

The Hawthorn or spring strainer is used in conjunction with the Boston shaker to strain ice from cocktails. This perforated strainer is fitted with a spring so it fits quickly and easily within the metal shaker lid. The spring creates equal resistance around the inside circumference of the rim to hold back ice when shaking a cocktail.

It is not ideal for cocktails that contain pieces of pulp, fiber, or mint, which are easily snagged in the spring. Most Hawthorn strainers are too large for use with the 16-ounce mixing glass.

Julep Strainer

A large perforated spoon, the julep strainer is so named because it is ideal for holding back large chunks of oversized mint not welcome in julep cocktails. It is used to strain cocktails made in the 16-ounce mixing glass, chiefly stirred cocktails. It should also be used to strain any cocktail that contains debris that would become snagged in a Hawthorn strainer.

Bar Spoon

A 12-inch-long spoon with a spiral twisted handle used for stirring, for handling garnishes, and as a measuring device. We recommend slightly curving or "bowing" the handle to make it easier to work with. With this adaptation, you can use it to move the whole amount of ice at once per revolution in the mixing glass. You may find some spoons fitted with a disk on the end, used for layering ingredients; you can also do this with the back of the bar spoon. Other spoons may have a plastic or metal knob on the end as a counterbalance; despite advertising claims, this does not work well for muddling.

Muddler

This large bar tool is used to crush fruits, herbs, and sugar. The best muddlers are fashioned in the shape of a baseball bat and are about 8 inches long—long enough to reach the bottom of the mixing glass. Muddlers come in wood, metal, and food-safe plastic. Wood is ideal because it has some give to it and you can really pulverize ingredients quickly and with force. Do not buy a painted muddler; with time, the paint will flake off into your cocktails. Beware of metal muddlers; they can easily shatter your mixing glass. Food-safe plastic is easy to clean and durable.

Jigger

The jigger is used for measuring liquid. Its design is specific to the small amounts of liquid required in making cocktails. The classic jigger is two stainless steel cones joined together at their points, in sizes ranging from ½ ounce to 2½ ounces. Today they come in all shapes and materials. Stainless steel jiggers are probably the most common to find and easy to clean. It does take some practice to use them quickly and efficiently.

Paring Knife

This short, sharp knife is used to cut garnishes. We recommend a blade of 4 inches, an ideal size that can be used with both small limes and large oranges. We use a straight blade that makes clean cuts rather than a serrated blade, although these are slightly safer to use as they more easily penetrate the skins of citrus fruit. Try both, and use the knife that you find safe, comfortable, and effective with your cutting style.

Demitasse Spoon

This small spoon is traditionally used with espresso. Its diminutive size makes it ideal for handling small, delicate garnishes. We also use a demitasse spoon as a measuring device for bar sugar, which some cocktails use in amounts smaller than 1 teaspoon. One heaping demitasse spoon is the equivalent of ½ teaspoon.

Citrus Zester

A citrus zester is used to cut long strips of zest from oranges or lemons. Most shapes have two functions: channel zester and zest grater. The channel zester is used to make a ribbon out of the peel; with skill, you can extend this for many inches by circling the fruit. This technique is also used by some to release oils over the drink without adding the actual peel as a garnish. The grater is used for making small threads of zest, primarily for cooking and dessert preparations.

Spice Grater

A spice grater is predominantly used to grate nutmeg and other spices over a poured cocktail. We recommend using a Microplane grater, which is a modern version of the classic tool that works more efficiently and is easier to clean.

Fine Sieve

Sieves become necessary when your cocktail recipe incorporates raw materials that should not end up in the final cocktail. A small fine sieve is used for double-straining out muddled pulp and fruit residue. A larger sieve or chinois is a conical sieve ideal for making large batches of infusions and syrups that require straining.

ICE AS A TOOL AND INGREDIENT

Ice in mixed drinks is often taken for granted. For the past few decades, the perception of ice has been related to profit. Restaurant and bar owners have recognized that smaller-shaped ice takes up more space and melts faster, resulting in greater dilution, hence less liquor going into drinks, resulting in increased profits. This view of ice as a way to take up volume has no place in proper cocktail making. Today the cocktail community recognizes ice as a critical component of a well-made cocktail. Seminars about ice are held at conferences and articles solely about ice appear in trade journals around the world. No need to bore you with an extended lesson on ice for the purposes of this book. Simply put, there is block ice, cubed ice, cracked ice or lump ice, crushed ice, and shaved ice.

Ice is a tool—possibly the most important tool in cocktail making. When shaken or stirred in drinks, ice (1) reduces the temperature and (2) imparts water into the cocktail. As chefs use a stove to cook food, bartenders use ice to chill. The size, shape, and temperature of your ice will directly influence the quality of your cocktails and mixed drinks. Some bars use different kinds of ice to apply different chilling techniques. The greater the ice-to-liquid ratio, the slower the dilution. This allows more time in the mixing glass, which results in colder cocktails. The ice in the ice cube trays in your freezer is roughly the size best suited for making cocktails. This all-purpose ice can be used for all cocktails and can be broken down by grinding or smashing. We recommend a minimum of 1-inch cubes for stirring and shaking cocktails, whether at home or behind a bar. The smaller ice cubes that most restaurants use melt too fast, watering down the powerful and delicate flavors found in crafted cocktails. Be wary of cocktail places that utilize those half-moon-shaped ice chips. This ice is terrible; it will melt in the palm of your hand in less than a minute. Remember that size leads to "meltage" or dilution from ice water. This water that makes its way into the cocktail plays a significant role in the taste of the final product. It binds all the ingredients together in a cocktail.

Use only fresh ice. Do not use the ice that has been sitting in your freezer from last year, last month, or even last week. Ice retains smells and aromas, so if you don't want your Manhattan cocktail to smell of pork ribs, make your ice no more than a day ahead. The best ice is so cold that it is dry and will stick to your fingers when touched. When the ice starts getting wet on the surface, it's a sure sign that its temperature is rising. Prepare a lot of ice. Remember this: no ice, no party.

Funnel

Stainless steel funnels are a necessity behind our busy bar, as many bar ingredients go into bottles with narrow openings. Plastic food-safe funnels are great, but stainless steel funnels are sleek and easier to clean.

Tongs

Tongs are used predominantly for handling ice, garnishes, and fruits. Although tongs look more professional, many ingredients require the use of one of a bartender's most important tools: the hands.

Building

When making cocktails, we refer to the process as *building* the cocktail. The primary technique used in building cocktails is pouring. At Employees Only, we practice a technique called "free pouring." Just as the term implies, this is pouring ingredients without the aid of a measuring device. This method is twofold: mechanical and technical. It requires skill in the way you hold the bottle, and order and building techniques also come into play. We recommend that you use all of your senses to build your cocktails accurately and efficiently. And we'll say it again: the only way to build your skill is with practice. Don't be afraid to try these techniques! They are quite fun and very rewarding.

Begin with the mechanics of holding the bottle. All of our bottles are fitted with pour spouts to help regulate and minimize the emerging stream of liquid. So it is important that you be able to "turn on" and "turn off" that stream quickly and maintain a constant, consistent stream. Hold the bottle at the neck, wrapping your index finger, middle finger, and thumb just below the pour spout. Many pour spouts have a small hole that lets air in. By covering this hole, you can stop the flow of liquid. Your grip on the bottle should be high enough to allow you to cover the air hole with your index finger. This is not necessary if you wield the bottle correctly. The motion of pouring is all in the wrist and shoulder and should radiate your elbow from your side to shoulder level. Quickly turn the bottle 170 degrees. Do not hesitate and do not be afraid to pour straight down. This will allow the liquid to be forced out at constant pressure, ensuring rhythmic flow. With your pouring hand, you should be able to feel the liquid pouring out as air comes into the bottle. To stop pouring, twist your wrist back and lower your arm, letting the weight of the bottom of the bottle do all the work. To perfect this, practice with a bottle of water fitted with a pour spout and a mixing glass. Once you pour confidently, you can continue to learn how to build cocktails.

The next step is accuracy. You must be able to pour the required measurements. To measure your cocktails, use your eyes. This is why we use the mixing glass when making cocktails. Memorize imaginary markers on the side of the glass for different amounts of liquids. Be sure to hold up the glass so you are looking through it, not over or below it. Do not rely on counting the time of your pours. Instant bartending schools preach the idea of "counts." Counts assume a standard rate of flow, but different liquors have different viscosities and so pour at different rates. And our concept of time changes from when things are calm to when they get hectic. That's why we suggest that you rely on your sense of sight. As you improve, you will be able to feel the liquid exiting the bottle with your pouring hand as well. These two senses together will help you develop your rhythm. Rhythm of flow is what "counts" are trying to achieve. If you need to count in your head, do so only to perfect your rhythm.

To build cocktails, some bartending guides instruct you to first pour the "flavoring agents," then the "modifiers," and finish with the "base spirit." In our opinion, these outdated terms and order have no importance. They try to mechanize the way that flavors and ingredients

work together. And notice that in this process the spirit is poured last, so if any mistakes are made, no precious booze is lost. When *all* your ingredients are precious, this mentality does not apply. Develop your own order to perfect your pouring technique. What is important is that your method allows you to best understand the relationship between the ingredients in the glass.

Stirring

Stirring is the oldest cocktail-making technique and a much gentler chilling method then shaking. Large cold ice cubes should be used in stirring, because this allows for a longer stirring time and thus a colder cocktail. Classics such

USING ALL YOUR SENSES

Experience will give you your touch for the amount of each ingredient and the final color. You can distinguish five different tastes: sweet, salty, tart, bitter, and astringent. On the other hand, your sense of smell can differentiate among anywhere from 2,000 to 2,500 different aromas. You shouldn't take mid-preparation tastes of the cocktails you prepare for someone else, but you can "nose" them. As you pour each ingredient into the mixing glass, nose it and see how each one affects the overall cocktail. Every ingredient should find

harmony in a cocktail, so you should be able to detect every ingredient in the mix. Smell every cocktail before shaking and smell it afterward. Smell the spirit on its own, then smell it when you add the accentuating or contrasting flavors. If these do not contribute, either you need to increase the amount of the flavor, or it does not belong in the cocktail. This exercise will enable you to pour cocktails with the sufficient amounts to precision. Mastering this technique will aid you when you begin conceiving your own cocktails.

as Gin Martinis, Manhattans, and Negronis should always be stirred. The old adage says that cocktails that contain only spirits, liquors, vermouths, and bitters are stirred; those that contain juices, fruits, and egg whites are shaken. Stirring creates a silky texture and luxurious marriage of ingredients in a cocktail. The flavors in the resulting cocktail will be as delicate and refined as the process itself. The technique of stirring is simple, but one master will instantly recognize another by the ease with which the other stirs.

Prepare the cocktail for stirring by pouring all the ingredients into a mixing glass. Next add ice to just below the rim of the glass. Now take your bar spoon. It should be slightly curved,

so when you place it into the mixing glass and start stirring it moves the whole amount of ice through the cocktail. Stir for about forty revolutions. Touch the sides of the mixing glass to feel how the temperature has dropped. You will know a cocktail is sufficiently chilled when it is cold to the touch. Remove the spoon and use the julep strainer to empty the contents into the intended glassware.

Examine the way you stir. If you look like a witch stirring a cauldron, you are not on the right track. Practice with an empty glass. Hold your hand above the glass and stir using solely the twist of your wrist; your hand should remain in the same hovering position. Move the spoon in circles so that the back is always touching the inner wall of the glass. Practice this at different levels in the glass until you have mastered the technique, then see how easy it is to accomplish with the ice.

Shaking

Shaking is used to aggressively chill a cocktail. Unlike stirring, shaking adds life and wakes up all the ingredients by incorporating air as well as water. When you shake a cocktail properly, you trap air in it, which dramatically affects its texture and the way the flavors reach your tongue. Ingredients like juices taste flat without shaking to bring them to life. Egg whites and pineapple juice are great for trapping a lot of air for a frothy creamy texture. Shaking can also add small pieces of ice to the cocktail.

To make a shaken cocktail, prepare your ingredients in the mixing glass. Add ice so that it mounds above the brim of the mixing glass. The quality of ice is extremely important (see page 17); large ice cubes melt more slowly, so you will need to shake them long and hard to add the right amount of water. You can use the Boston shaker to scoop the maximum amount of ice that will fit into the cocktail. Hold the mixing glass on a sturdy surface in one hand, and close the metal shaker over the top on an angle. Smack the bottom of the metal shaker to create a tight seal. You should see from one side that the shaker and mixing glass form a straight line and that the top and bottom of the assembly will not be parallel. You should be able to pick up the cocktail by the bottom of the shaker without breaking the seal.

Now flip the assembly around with the shaker on the bottom in your left hand and the mixing glass on top in your right hand, with your middle finger filling the gap between the metal rim and the glass. Lift the shaker; place it parallel to the line going straight from your right ear to your right eye.

It is very important to shake the cocktail as hard as you can. Start shaking in a steady, but very aggressive rhythm. The contents should smack from end to end, making sharp, loud noises.

Shaking time depends on the size of the ice—as noted earlier, larger cubes will take longer to melt, so an average shake time with good ice should last six to ten seconds. When you're through shaking, set down the shaker and pull out the mixing glass (see "Opening the Seal," page 22). Holding a Hawthorn strainer over the top of the shaker, pour the cocktail into the waiting glass.

Muddling

Muddling is a cocktail-making process used to crush fruits, herbs, and sugar, extracting aromatic and essential oils from the peels and skins of citrus fruits and blending together all of the muddled ingredients. Muddling is done in the bottom of a mixing glass with a muddler (see page 16), which allows you to apply the necessary pressure to pulverize the ingredients. Be sure that the glass in which you are muddling is sturdy enough for the process. Also note that many muddled drinks require sugar as well to sweeten the fruit or vegetable. Sugar is a great

OPENING THE SEAL

The Boston shaker closes properly around the mixing glass at a specific angle range of 15 to 20 degrees. It creates a very tight seal that holds the shaker closed. The metal part of the shaker will shrink more in the shaking; it is an excellent conductor of heat and cold, and the ice makes the metal colder and therefore tighter. So sometimes it's very hard to open this seal, even for an experienced bartender. Some people think they can dislodge the glass by just hitting it hard against something. Bad idea! There is actually an easy method that takes just a little practice to master.

When looking at the assembly from above, turn your shaker so that the mixing glass points "north." At due "east" and "west" you will notice a slight gap forming between the metal shaker and the mixing glass. This is the sweet spot for releasing the seal. You can do so by lightly hitting the heel of your palm on the outside of the shaker right at that point. It works because this quick pressure applied to the malleable metal shaker changes its shape slightly from the shape of the glass rim; air slips through and releases the seal. Practice this, and with a few attempts you will get your own feel for how to open the seal. Be patient, and whatever you do, do not try to open the seal by banging the whole contraption on the bar top, refrigeration equipment, or yourself. This can lead to broken glass and stitches.

tool to muddle with because it provides grip while you're working, like sandpaper to wear down the ingredient.

Layering and Floating

Layering and floating are techniques not frequently used in modern bartending, but they have their place and are definitely an important part of your skill set. These techniques involve slow pouring of liquids over the back of the bar spoon, thus layering "lighter" or less dense liquids on top of denser ones. The layered drink is also called a pousse-café. We find examples in cocktails like the B-52 and the Black and Tan.

ABOUT THE RECIPES

The recipes in this book are organized to give you a greater understanding of the cocktails before you make them. Each recipe contains information that will help you appreciate the cocktail's origins as well as its ingredients and how they work together. First, we tell the story of the drink. Tasting notes help you decide whether a cocktail is to your liking and also understand what is happening in the glass. We suggest glassware and ingredients to help create the experience we offer at Employees Only. We tell how to make the drink properly using the techniques already described. As first noted in the introduction, you'll sometimes find related sets: an original EO cocktail (or cocktails) followed by the classic (or classics) that gave us inspiration. The ↡ symbol distinguishes our EO recipes—look for it in the recipe titles. The classic recipes indicate the influences that went into our cocktail-creating process. While not every

drink is a riff on a classic, no drink was born out of a vacuum either. The recipes are grouped to help illustrate how one can reimagine cocktails.

EVERY COCKTAIL HAS A STORY

Like wine, every cocktail has its own story and purpose for being in the world. Most cocktails we refer to as classics carry with them stories—a few of which reach mythological proportions. There are anecdotes about the names, accidental inceptions, and tales of their rise to fame. Even if they are not true, stories help people remember and identify with a cocktail. Stories are very important to the fulfillment of the guest's experience. We would even go so far as to claim that stories make cocktails taste better. Stories help us sell cocktails every night at the bar. We leave the truth to the cocktail historians who debunk the information that was handed down to us. For some, the real story turns out to be more outlandish than the lie. For others, the birth remains shrouded in mystery. Cocktailians such as David Wondrich have written wonderful material about the subject. In this book, we share stories of recipes that have intrigued us. Accuracy is not the point; they are good stories. That said, it is imperative that you research, read, and educate yourself about all the facts that will enable you to give your guests an experience.

TASTING NOTES

In the past, the ingredients of cocktails were broken down into base, modifier, and flavoring agent. Essentially this breakdown represents the base spirit, the juice or vermouth, and the cordial, respectively. It does nothing to illustrate how the cocktail comes together or how it feels. Often, many flavors overlap between these distinctions, blurring the lines of this rigid definition. We have done away with this archaic system and redefined what makes up a cocktail. For each recipe, we have provided tasting notes that represent our experience tasting each cocktail. There is little existing vocabulary for this, so we have created one, borrowing from the languages of both the wine and the culinary worlds to describe the aromas, flavors, and textures, as follows:

- *Dominant flavors.* These flavors exemplify what the cocktail "should be." In many cases it is the spirit forward, like gin in a Martini or the whiskey in a Sazerac; in others it is the obvious muddled fruits.

- *Body.* This element represents the texture of the cocktail—its mouthfeel. Sometimes it will have pieces of fruit or debris; other times, it will be silky smooth. Egg whites trap a lot of air, as in a soufflé. Air molecules create textural sensations in the mouth. Sweeteners also affect the body by increasing richness and viscosity. Intense flavors may also contribute to a fuller body. High alcohol content creates a full-bodied impression.

- *Dryness.* Borrowed from the wine lexicon, "dryness" serves as an antonym for the term "sweet." Cocktails created by professionals should never be only sweet. Although they may be on the sweet side, there should be balance among the notes of sourness, bitterness, or alcohol. Sugar and other sweeteners

help to decrease dryness. Acidic ingredients such as citrus fruits help increase dryness, as do tannins in teas and wines.

- *Complexity.* This refers to richness—the depth of layers in a cocktail, measured from low to high. Complexity may be subtle, coming out only in the finish, or be amazingly bold and up front. Cocktails that incorporate simple straightforward flavors have low complexity. Bitters often enrich complexity. Gin is an excellent vehicle for cocktails with subtle complexity. Other ingredients that increase complexity are absinthes, fernets, vermouths, amaros, Benedictine, and the Chartreuse liqueurs.

- *Accentuating or contrasting flavors.* Our cocktails are more than just a balance between spirit and juices or cordials. To create three-dimensional cocktails, there must be an element that makes the cocktail "pop." Accentuating flavors usually increase one dominant flavor while filling a void in body or complexity. Flavors that contrast with a dominant flavor add greater depth. Bitters are commonly used to contrast with the fruit-forward flavors found in tropical cocktails. Creative cocktail makers take a culinary approach, learning, for example, that fresh berries and gin seem to pair well, as do whiskey and stone fruits. When using citrus juices to accentuate fruit flavors, the rule of lemon for "old world fruits" and lime for exotic or tropical fruits works well.

- *Finish.* When you swallow the cocktail, the taste sensation you experience is called the finish. As with wine, this can be short, dry, or even lingering. The finish is often provided by essential oils found in bitters and twists. A crisp finish may come from the acid in citrus. Tannic items may also create a lip-smacking, lingering finish. High alcohol content will greatly affect the finish.

GLASSWARE

The look of the cocktail is almost as important as its flavor. For this reason, cocktails should look stunning, with proper glassware and garnishing. Glassware not only affects the visual style of the drink but also can enhance its flavor. Champagne coupes (the older saucer-shaped glasses) and cocktail glasses allow for a larger surface area of aromas to reach the nose, thus enhancing the experience of an aromatic cocktail. At Employees Only, we use streamlined rocks and Collins glasses to fit in with our Art Deco décor. Our signature cocktail glass—an oversized champagne coupe—gives the cocktails a context in time. This selection also ensures that people do not confuse us with a Martini bar. Each recipe suggests the appropriate glassware. If you wish to substitute with glasses you have, remember that rocks glasses are short and stout, Collins glasses are tall and narrow, and cocktail glasses have a wide surface area to expose the aromas.

GARNISHES

Since the birth of the cocktail, when the first Sazeracs were made in New Orleans, bartenders have used garnishes to add flavor, color, and a decorative accent to the cocktail. Don't underestimate the importance of the garnish; it not only adds a culinary note, but the moment you add it signals the guest that the cocktail is ready to be enjoyed. The garnish should never be arbitrary—it should have some clear kinship with the cocktail flavors, whether to accompany or to contrast.

APERITIFS

T HE APERITIF IS THE FIRST DRINK OF THE EVENING, the appetizer of the cocktail world that is enjoyed prior to the meal and often alongside hors d'oeuvres or appetizers. Aperitifs tend to be strong in alcohol and often contain botanicals and bitter ingredients. One aperitif is perfect on an empty stomach, but too many can lead to an unpleasant evening. Their high alcohol content and robust character overpower most food, and their subtle complexities are best enjoyed on their own.

What we are calling "aperitifs" here falls under the style of drinks once known simply as cocktails. They follow the oldest definition known for a cocktail that appeared in the May 13, 1806, issue of the *Balance and Columbian Repository*:

Cocktail is a stimulating liquor composed of spirits of any kind, sugar, water, and bitters— it is vulgarly called a bittered sling and is supposed to be an excellent electioneering potion, inasmuch as it renders the heart stout and bold, at the same time that it fuddles the head. It is said, also to be of great use to a Democratic candidate: because a person, having swallowed a glass of it, is ready to swallow anything else.

Of course, the definition of "cocktail" has been broadened over some two hundred years to refer to a whole host of libations using juices, egg whites, fresh fruit, sodas, and purées, as more ingredients were added to bartenders' repertoires. To help readers understand the style of the cocktails to follow, we decided to create this subcategory of *aperitifs*. Overall, they are lighter in sugar and contain little or no fruit juices. The aperitif cocktail is the ultimate expression of a bartender's skill in blending and balancing subtle nuances against more pronounced flavors.

APEROL SPRITZ

The light and fizzy Spritz is a traditional Italian cocktail. It was typically enjoyed by older men playing cards in outdoor cafes. Here, we use Aperol, a gentle Italian aperitif with an alcohol content of 11 percent and a bittersweet flavor that comes from a careful balance of herbs, roots, bitter orange, and rhubarb. Brut Prosecco provides great acidity and a clean finish. Originally the Spritz was served in a wineglass, but at Employees Only we serve it tall to retain and concentrate the bubbles.   MAKES 1 DRINK

4½ ounces brut Prosecco

2½ ounces Aperol

1 lime wheel, for garnish

1 ounce club soda

Fill a Collins glass with ice. Pour the Prosecco over the large cold ice cubes. Add the Aperol and lime wheel and top off with the club soda.

Tasting Notes

DOMINANT FLAVORS: bitter orange and rhubarb
BODY: light, effervescent
DRYNESS: medium
COMPLEXITY: medium

ACCENTUATING OR CONTRASTING FLAVORS: acidity from the Prosecco and lime shining through
FINISH: short, snappy, bittersweet

GLASS: Collins

CAMPARI SPRITZ

The Campari Spritz is the predecessor of the Aperol Spritz. Whereas the Aperol version is soft, the Campari version is bold and assertive, so it is served in a smaller rocks glass and garnished with one large green olive. With its robust nature, the Campari Spritz is a very popular aperitivo *alongside various antipasti containing olive oil, spices, fresh mozzarella, and seafood such as octopus, calamari, and clams.*   MAKES 1 DRINK

2 ounces brut Prosecco

1 ounce club soda

2 ounces Campari

1 large green olive, for garnish

Build the cocktail carefully in a rocks glass over large cold ice cubes by first pouring the Prosecco. Add the club soda and finish with the Campari. Stir gently and garnish with the olive.

DOMINANT FLAVORS: herbs and tree bark
BODY: light, slightly effervescent
DRYNESS: medium to dry
COMPLEXITY: medium

ACCENTUATING OR CONTRASTING FLAVORS: rounded out by slight acidity
FINISH: short, bitter

GLASS: rocks

Tasting Notes

ELDERFLOWER SPRITZ

The Elderflower Spritz is EO's version of the St-Germain cocktail invented by Robert Cooper, the creator of St-Germain liqueur. The difference is that we add lemon slices for citrus in the middle. Our recipe was developed as a French version of the Italian Spritz, to offer to guests who dislike the bitterness of Aperol. Its flowery essence is calming and soothing, with a welcome simplicity. MAKES 1 DRINK

4 ounces Perrier-Jouët Grand Brut champagne

2 ounces St-Germain elderflower liqueur

2 ounces club soda

3 thinly sliced lemon wheels

Fill a large wine goblet with ice. Carefully pour the champagne over the large cold ice cubes, followed by the St-Germain, and finish with the club soda. Add the lemon wheels and stir slightly.

Tasting Notes

DOMINANT FLAVORS: floral with pear and grapefruit
BODY: light, effervescent
DRYNESS: medium to off-dry
COMPLEXITY: low

ACCENTUATING OR CONTRASTING FLAVORS: summer fruits like apricot from the champagne against citrus
FINISH: short, sweet

GLASS: large wine goblet

FERNANDO

This original EO aperitif pays tribute to Italian gastronomy. Its main ingredient, Fernet Branca—made of overly bitter barks, herbs, and spices—is traditionally served as a digestive, but it is rarely used in cocktails because it tends to overpower all other ingredients. Fernet is purported to be a cure-all for many ailments—upset stomachs, menstrual cramps, baby colic, even cholera. It is an acquired taste, which makes it the favorite shot of bartenders who gravitate toward flavors rejected by the general public. The Fernando is rich and chocolaty, slightly sweet, with a bitter finish. To complete the cocktail, the bartender smacks a fresh mint sprig in the palm of the hand to release the essential mint oils. This cocktail is ideal for Negroni drinkers and diehard fans of Fernet alike. MAKES 1 DRINK

1¼ ounces Fernet Branca

1¾ ounces Cinzano Bianco vermouth

¾ ounce Liquore Galliano

1 mint sprig, for garnish

Pour all the liquid ingredients into a mixing glass. Add large cold ice cubes and stir for 40 revolutions. Strain into a chilled cocktail glass. Place the fresh mint sprig in the palm of your hand and smack it with your other hand to release the aroma. Gently place the mint on the surface of the cocktail and serve.

DOMINANT FLAVORS: chocolate overtones and well-balanced botanicals

BODY: silky, rich

DRYNESS: medium

COMPLEXITY: high

ACCENTUATING OR CONTRASTING FLAVORS: vanilla and mint

FINISH: long, bitter, minty

GLASS: cocktail

Tasting Notes

MANHATTAN COCKTAIL

The Manhattan cocktail we serve is not to be confused with the contemporary Manhattan. This recipe first appeared in the latter part of the nineteenth century and is referenced in later editions of How to Mix Drinks or the Bon Vivant's Companion *as well as Harry Johnson's 1882* Bartenders' Manual. *This forgotten formula has a higher ratio of sweet vermouth to rye whiskey, with an accent of orange Curaçao and Boker's bitters, served straight up with a lemon twist. Cherries in Manhattans came later as the mixture evolved into a different cocktail. The subtle mingling of flavors in this version illustrates an older style of drink making.*

Of course, as with any epic cocktail, there are several conflicting stories about its origins. Our favorite version has Winston Churchill's mother, Jennie, ordering its creation for the celebration of Samuel Tilden's election as governor of New York at the Manhattan Club. As exciting as this may sound, it seems that little Winston had more to do with disproving the theory. At the time of the election, Lady Churchill was in England giving birth to Winston, and the only noted celebration for Tilden actually coincided with the day of Winston Churchill's christening. MAKES 1 DRINK

1½ ounces Rittenhouse 100-proof rye whiskey

1¾ ounces Dolin Rouge sweet vermouth

½ ounce Grand Marnier

3 dashes Angostura bitters

1 lemon twist, for garnish

Pour the whiskey, vermouth, liqueur, and bitters into a mixing glass. Add large cold ice cubes and stir for 40 revolutions. Strain into a chilled cocktail glass. Garnish with the lemon twist.

Tasting Notes

DOMINANT FLAVORS: rye whiskey with citrus on the nose
BODY: full with high alcohol content
DRYNESS: medium
COMPLEXITY: medium to high with perfect balance

ACCENTUATING OR CONTRASTING FLAVORS: soft botanicals in the vermouth against spicy bitters
FINISH: medium with oak and bittersweet orange overtones

GLASS: cocktail

CONTEMPORARY MANHATTAN

Most people today understand a Manhattan to be bourbon whiskey with a dash of vermouth, shaken or stirred—little more than a nice way to order a big shot of whiskey. Only recently have people once again acknowledged the necessity of bitters in the recipe. What happened?

Prohibition all but annihilated rye whiskey production in this country; by the end of World War II, America had embraced Canadian whiskies as rye, even though most are made of a blend of grains. When we first began bartending, it was common for Manhattans to be made with Seagram's VO or Crown Royal. But in the early 1990s, bartenders making Manhattans gravitated toward newly released single-barrel and small-batch bourbons to meet the expectations of the luxury crowd. As with Martinis, these customers demanded only a whisper of vermouth so as not to destroy the precious whiskey.

Our recipe is an excellent expression of a Manhattan made with soft-natured bourbon. Rye whiskey makes a sharp, racy alternative. As for cherries, keep clear of the big artificial ones floating in eerie red dye. Pit fresh cherries and soak them for a few days in amaretto or cherry liqueur instead. MAKES 1 DRINK

3 ounces Woodford Reserve 90-proof bourbon

1½ ounces Dolin Rouge sweet vermouth

3 dashes Angostura bitters

3 brandied cherries, for garnish

Pour the bourbon, vermouth, and bitters into a mixing glass. Add large cold ice cubes and stir for 40 revolutions. Strain into a chilled cocktail glass. Garnish with the cherries.

Tasting Notes

DOMINANT FLAVORS: bourbon all over
BODY: full, with high alcohol content
DRYNESS: dry
COMPLEXITY: low to medium

ACCENTUATING OR CONTRASTING FLAVORS: bitters working well with botanicals from sweet vermouth
FINISH: short, dry with sweet corn and slight vanilla overtones

GLASS: cocktail

In the mythology of classic mixology, the Martinez is purported to be the predecessor to the Dry Gin Martini. When we researched the original version of this cocktail, though, we saw very little resemblance to what people today refer to as a Martini. In an act of artistic interpretation, we devised a recipe to be the "missing link" to articulate the evolution of these two iconic cocktails. In doing so, we created a more dry—and more exciting—flavor profile than that of the original Martinez. Our missing link provides an experience with a beginning, middle, and finish that lingers, leaving you craving more. This is best achieved with the combination of Beefeater 24 gin, accents of maraschino liqueur, and the super velvetiness of Dolin Blanc vermouth. Finally, our own homemade Absinthe Bitters round it out and add incredible depth. This drink has been offered on our aperitif menu since we opened Employees Only. It goes great with raw oysters or raw bar of any kind and works well with summery salads and seared scallops. MAKES 1 DRINK

2½ ounces Beefeater 24 gin

½ ounce Luxardo maraschino liqueur

¾ ounce Dolin Blanc vermouth

¼ ounce Absinthe Bitters (page 184)

1 lemon twist, for garnish

Pour all the liquid ingredients into a mixing glass. Add large cold ice cubes and stir for 40 revolutions. Strain into a chilled cocktail glass. Garnish with the lemon twist.

DOMINANT FLAVORS: juniper, anise, maraschino
BODY: silken texture created by the combination of blanc vermouth and maraschino
DRYNESS: medium

COMPLEXITY: high
ACCENTUATING OR CONTRASTING FLAVORS: absinthe bitters
FINISH: green tea, lingering sweet anise

GLASS: cocktail

Tasting Notes

CLASSIC MARTINEZ

Whether or not this drink is truly an ancestor of today's Dry Gin Martini (with which it has little in common), it is a great model in the cocktail fossil record because it showcases how certain ingredients were used before the twentieth century: back in the day, maraschino liqueur and orange Curaçao were two cordials used interchangeably (depending on availability) as sweeteners in cocktails. Vermouth was always sweet Italian red vermouth; French or dry vermouth were not popular in cocktail making until the end of the nineteenth century. Legend says this drink was named for the small Northern California town where a Gold Rush miner ordered "one for the road" before heading for the hills. MAKES 1 DRINK

1¾ ounces Beefeater London Dry gin

2 ounces Dolin Rouge sweet vermouth

¼ ounce Luxardo maraschino liqueur

1 dash Regan's Orange Bitters No. 6

1 lemon twist, for garnish

Pour all the liquid ingredients into a mixing glass. Add large cold ice cubes and stir for 40 revolutions. Strain into a chilled cocktail glass. Garnish with the lemon twist.

Tasting Notes

DOMINANT FLAVORS: juniper, maraschino, caramel
BODY: velvety texture created by the combination of Italian vermouth and maraschino
DRYNESS: medium to sweet
COMPLEXITY: high

ACCENTUATING OR CONTRASTING FLAVORS: maraschino and herbs
FINISH: medium, fragrant

GLASS: cocktail

NERINA

This EO original aperitif (see photo on page 43) was inspired by the Negroni cocktail (page 42). It is a great example of how elegant and complex three liquids blended in a cocktail can be. Its rich flavors come from amaro, which we use in place of Campari, and Punt e Mes, in place of traditional sweet vermouth. Amaro is a bitter Italian digestif made from herbs and plants; for the Nerina, we prefer Meletti amaro, which has a beautiful spice profile with lingering notes of cinnamon, but is light on caramel compared to other amaros. Punt e Mes is a highly bittersweet aromatized wine, considered by some to be the original of Italian vermouth. Combined and blended with gin, the ingredients create a cocktail of simple sophistication. The name is a nod to the classic Negroni cocktail. Being a dark–hued drink, Nerina *comes from* nera, *the feminine Italian word for black.* MAKES 1 DRINK

1¼ ounces Plymouth gin

1¼ ounces Meletti amaro

1¼ ounces Punt e Mes sweet vermouth

1 orange twist, for garnish

Pour all the liquid ingredients into a mixing glass. Add large cold ice cubes and stir for 40 revolutions. Strain into a chilled cocktail glass. Garnish with the orange twist.

DOMINANT FLAVORS: juniper, cinnamon, caramel, and orange on the nose
BODY: velvety
DRYNESS: medium
COMPLEXITY: high

ACCENTUATING OR CONTRASTING FLAVORS: blend of herbs and spices
FINISH: short, spicy with caramel overtones

GLASS: cocktail

Tasting Notes

NEGRONI

The Negroni is the favorite classic cocktail of the EO bar staff. It is said that every bartender eventually has an affair with the Negroni. It is the Mrs. Robinson of cocktails—stunning, sexy, and mature. Its dark, alluring color is only a preview for the bittersweet aromas that blossom on the palate.

Many bartenders pay homage to this cocktail style, trying to coax complexity out of just a few simple elements. It is said that this drink was first created in Florence in 1919 for Count Camillo Negroni, who insisted upon adding a kick to his Americano cocktail. The bartender substituted gin for the club soda, and a legend was born. The Negroni was classically served on the rocks but was adapted to be served straight up to prevent the flavors from being watered down. MAKES 1 DRINK

1¼ ounces Plymouth gin

1¼ ounces Campari

1¼ ounces Cinzano sweet vermouth

1 orange twist or half-wheel, for garnish

Pour all the liquid ingredients into a mixing glass. Add large cold ice cubes and stir for 40 revolutions. Strain into a chilled cocktail glass and garnish with an orange twist. Or strain into an ice-filled rocks glass and garnish with an orange half-wheel.

Tasting Notes

DOMINANT FLAVORS: juniper, quinine, orange, and rhubarb

BODY: silky texture, medium

DRYNESS: medium to dry

COMPLEXITY: high

ACCENTUATING OR CONTRASTING FLAVORS: herbs versus spices

FINISH: long, bitter

GLASS: cocktail or rocks

LEFT TO RIGHT: Negroni, Tifozi (page 44), Nerina (page 41)

TIFOZI

The term "tifozi" is slang used to describe hardcore Italian soccer fans, and there is nothing more hardcore Italian than this aperitivo. The Tifozi (see photo on page 43) is an EO original based on the Americano cocktail (opposite), intended to be a humorous salute to its namesake. It is bitter, sweet, sour, and fizzy with the addition of San Pellegrino Aranciata, a natural orange-flavored soda. The lime wheels add freshness and life to the cocktail.   MAKES 1 DRINK

1½ ounces Campari

1½ ounces Punt e Mes sweet vermouth

3 lime wheels

3 ounces San Pellegrino Aranciata

Pour the Campari and vermouth into a Collins glass. Add large cold ice cubes and the lime wheels. Cover the glass with a small shaker and shake gently. Top off with the Aranciata.

Tasting Notes

DOMINANT FLAVORS: bitter fruits and sweet citrus with orange on the nose

BODY: light, effervescent

DRYNESS: medium

COMPLEXITY: medium

ACCENTUATING OR CONTRASTING FLAVORS: bitter botanicals from the Campari

FINISH: medium, semisweet

GLASS: Collins

AMERICANO

The Americano is the quintessential Italian aperitivo. When it was first created at Gaspare Campari's bar in Milan in the 1860s, it was named Milano-Torino for its two main ingredients: Campari from Milan and Cinzano from Turin. The drink quickly became popular as an afternoon quencher at outdoor caffès in the Italian piazzas. The name changed during Prohibition due to the mass of thirsty American tourists who fell in love with it. Some fifty years later, this drink would inspire one of the most fantastic aperitifs ever: the Negroni (page 42). It is little noted that the Americano is the first cocktail that James Bond orders in Ian Fleming's first novel Casino Royale, *long before he orders a Martini.*   MAKES 1 DRINK

1½ ounces Campari

1½ ounces Dolin Rouge sweet vermouth

1 orange half-wheel

3 ounces chilled club soda

Pour the Campari and vermouth into a Collins glass. Add large cold ice cubes and the orange half-wheel. Cover the glass with a small shaker and shake gently. Top off with the club soda.

DOMINANT FLAVORS: bitter fruits and subtle spices
BODY: light, effervescent
DRYNESS: dry
COMPLEXITY: medium

ACCENTUATING OR CONTRASTING FLAVORS: surprising sweetness contrasting bitter flavors with undertones of herbs and botanicals
FINISH: medium, bittersweet

GLASS: Collins

Tasting Notes

PÊCHE BOURBON

Pêche bourbon *is simply the French way of saying "peach bourbon." These two items are as compatible a pairing as strawberries and vanilla. We wanted to showcase our peach-infused bourbon without overshadowing any of its subtle beauty. We blended it in the most straightforward way, with sugar and Peychaud's bitters, then followed the ritual used to make the classic Sazerac cocktail (opposite): we first "season" the serving glass with French peach cordial. The ingredients swirl together in a slow dance, exciting the palate, then leaving it longing for more. This is a very delicate yet powerful cocktail. It is a great aperitif; it pairs well with grilled meats and seafood; and it is sublime as an after-dinner drink with a fruit tart or cake.* MAKES 1 DRINK

½ ounce Massenez crème de pêche or peach liqueur

1 raw brown sugar cube

½ teaspoon superfine sugar

3 dashes Peychaud's bitters

3 dashes Fee Brothers peach bitters

2 ounces Peach-Infused Bourbon (page 160)

1 mint sprig, for garnish

Pour the crème de pêche into a rocks glass. Swirl it around until the inside of the glass is completely coated, then discard the excess. Place in the freezer to chill. Place the sugars in the bottom of a mixing glass and saturate them with the Peychaud's and peach bitters. Muddle the sugars and bitters into a consistent paste. Add the bourbon and stir gently. Add large cold ice cubes and stir for 40 revolutions. Strain into the seasoned rocks glass. Place the mint sprig in the palm of your hand and smack it with your other hand to release the aroma. Gently place the mint on the surface of the cocktail and serve.

Tasting Notes

DOMINANT FLAVORS: whiskey and mint on the nose
BODY: full with high alcohol content
DRYNESS: medium
COMPLEXITY: high

ACCENTUATING OR CONTRASTING FLAVORS: peaches, peaches, peaches, with little spice
FINISH: medium, sweet, peachy

GLASS: rocks

SAZERAC

The Sazerac was invented by pharmacist Antoine Amedee Peychaud in New Orleans sometime in the early 1800s. In his French Quarter drugstore, M. Peychaud served his concoction of Sazerac cognac, absinthe, sugar, and his homemade bitters in the large end of an egg cup—what the French call a coquetier. *(There had been speculation that the word* cocktail *comes from the mispronunciation of* coquetier, *but this myth has been disproven.) Later, rye whiskey replaced Sazerac cognac because it was more readily available, but the name stayed.*

The traditional making of a Sazerac is a ritual still practiced in New Orleans. It begins with the bartender pouring Herbsaint into a rocks glass, then tossing the glass in the air while yelling "Sazerac!" Coating the inside of a glass with liquor is referred to as "seasoning" the glass. The glass is then chilled as the cocktail is made. At Employees Only, we make Sazeracs by seasoning the glass with our Absinthe Bitters, and we use Angostura bitters in addition to Peychaud's. MAKES 1 DRINK

¼ ounce Absinthe Bitters (page 161)

1 raw brown sugar cube

½ teaspoon superfine sugar

3 dashes Peychaud's bitters

1 dash Angostura bitters

2½ ounces Rittenhouse 100-proof rye whiskey

1 lemon twist, for garnish

Pour the Absinthe Bitters into a rocks glass. Swirl it around until the inside of the glass is completely coated, then discard the excess. Place in the freezer to chill. Place both sugars in the bottom of a mixing glass and saturate them with the Peychaud's and Angostura bitters. Muddle the sugars and bitters into a consistent paste. Add the whiskey and stir gently. Add large cold ice cubes and stir for 40 revolutions. Strain into the seasoned rocks glass and garnish with a lemon twist.

DOMINANT FLAVORS: whiskey with citrus on the nose
BODY: full with high alcohol content
DRYNESS: medium
COMPLEXITY: high with subtle complexity

ACCENTUATING OR CONTRASTING FLAVORS: anise with spices from bitters coating the whiskey
FINISH: lingering with anise overtones

GLASS: rocks

Tasting Notes

The Provençal is Employees Only's most romantic original aperitif and a seductive start to an intimate dinner. Mouthwatering, sexy, and savory, it was created as a pairing for raw oysters to heighten the sensual experience. After years of watching certain cocktails being erroneously labeled "Martinis," we felt the need to get back to the roots of the Martini and create a gin and vermouth concoction. We use lavender-infused Plymouth gin and French dry vermouth scented with herbes de Provence and blend them with Cointreau to give the Provençal its unique appearance and flavor. We hoped it would rival the standard dry Martini as the predinner cocktail, and it exceeded all expectations. The Provençal is a tribute to the golden age of cocktails when bartenders made many of their own ingredients in-house—it is the archetypical EO aperitif. Both the gin and vermouth infusions are easy to make, and the results are truly extraordinary.   MAKES 1 DRINK

2 ounces Lavender-Infused Gin (page 160)

1¼ ounces Vermouth de Provence (page 158)

¾ ounce Cointreau

1 orange twist, for garnish

Pour the gin, vermouth, and Cointreau into a mixing glass. Add large cold ice cubes and stir for 40 revolutions. Strain into a chilled cocktail glass. Garnish with the orange twist.

DOMINANT FLAVORS: lavender and juniper with orange on the nose

BODY: velvety mouthfeel, high alcohol content

DRYNESS: medium with sharp acidity from rosemary and thyme

COMPLEXITY: high

ACCENTUATING OR CONTRASTING FLAVORS: herbal contrast against soft lavender flavors

FINISH: long, herbal with sharp orange oil overtones

GLASS: cocktail

Tasting Notes

CLASSIC DRY MARTINI

The majesty of cocktails, the Martini is the most iconic mixed drink in the world. The name itself conjures up an image of the V-shaped cocktail glass with an olive resting in its depth. There is much debate about the origin of this drink. What is not in question is that this cocktail has evolved over time. Its simplicity is an illusion: the dry Martini takes years to master. The clear stillness and serenity of the final drink is an expression of the years of skill and experience of the person stirring it, and the proper execution of this cocktail is an exercise in honing the craft of cocktail making. MAKES 1 DRINK

3½ ounces Beefeater London Dry gin

½ ounce Dolin Dry vermouth

1 dash Regan's Orange Bitters No. 6

1 lemon twist, for garnish

Pour the gin, vermouth, and bitters into a mixing glass. Add large cold ice cubes and stir for 40 revolutions. Strain into a chilled cocktail glass. Garnish with the lemon twist.

Tasting Notes

DOMINANT FLAVORS: juniper and citrus oil
BODY: silky texture, clean mouthfeel
DRYNESS: very dry
COMPLEXITY: medium with many subtle aromatics

ACCENTUATING OR CONTRASTING FLAVORS: slight acidity from vermouth
FINISH: lingering with citrus oil overtones

GLASS: cocktail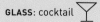

VESPER

The original recipe for the Vesper was created not by a bartender but by popular spy novelist Ian Fleming. In Fleming's 1953 book Casino Royale, *Agent 007 instructs the bartender to prepare him a Martini with "Three measures of Gordon's, one of vodka, half a measure of Kina Lillet. Shake it very well until it's ice cold, then add a large, thin slice of lemon." Bond named this drink after Vesper Lynd, his first love interest in the series. Kina Lillet vermouth, with its flavor notes of quinine, no longer exists, so we replaced it with Lillet Blanc and a dash of Angostura bitters. We opted for a blend of Charbay clear vodka and Plymouth Navy Strength gin to finish off our interpretation. This is the cocktail that introduced the phrase "shaken, not stirred," which changed Martini drinking forever. Thank you, Mr. Bond.* MAKES 1 DRINK

2 ounces Charbay vodka

1 ounce Plymouth Navy Strength gin

¾ ounce Lillet Blanc

1 dash Angostura bitters

1 lemon twist, for garnish

Pour the vodka, gin, Lillet Blanc, and bitters into a mixing glass. Add large cold ice cubes and shake vigorously. Strain into a chilled cocktail glass. Garnish with the lemon twist.

Tasting Notes

DOMINANT FLAVORS: clean citrus and light botanicals
BODY: ice cold, mellow
DRYNESS: dry
COMPLEXITY: low with straightforward flavors

ACCENTUATING OR CONTRASTING FLAVORS: slight acidity and fruit from vermouth
FINISH: short, mouth-cleansing with hint of orange

GLASS: cocktail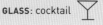

SECRET CRUSH

This cocktail is an Employees Only variation on the Champagne Cocktail (page 56). In champagne production, when the pinot noir skins are left to touch the juice, they add color and a soft touch of tannins. The result is some of the best aperitif wine available: rosé champagne. Other sparkling wine producers emulate this with rosé varietals, most notably the Spanish with Cava. These wines are truly magnificent, and their affordability makes them very suitable for mixed drinks. Cava rosé has a body and level of dryness ideal for adding sugar, bitters, and Campari to create a sultry variation on the classic Champagne Cocktail. This cocktail is very sexy and inviting and makes a superb aperitif, as well as a great choice for pairing with antipasti, mezes, tapas, or seafood appetizers. MAKES 1 DRINK

5 ounces Llopart Cava Leopardi brut rosé, divided

1 raw brown sugar cube

4 or 5 dashes Angostura bitters

¾ ounce Campari

1 lemon twist

Pour 1½ ounces of the sparkling wine into a champagne flute. Place the sugar cube on a bar spoon and saturate it with the bitters. Carefully place the sugar cube in the flute. Let rest for a moment. Pour in the rest of the sparkling wine. Add the Campari. Twist the lemon peel over the drink, then discard.

DOMINANT FLAVORS: floral and rose petals
BODY: light, effervescent
DRYNESS: dry, crisp
COMPLEXITY: low

ACCENTUATING OR CONTRASTING FLAVORS: bitterness from the Campari
FINISH: long, bitter

GLASS: champagne flute

Tasting Notes

CHAMPAGNE COCKTAIL

The recipe for this cocktail appeared in the first 1862 edition of Jerry Thomas's How to Mix Drinks or the Bon Vivant's Companion. *The original recipe illustrates the simplest incarnation of the cocktail in general: spirits or wines mixed with sugar, bitters, and water. Over the years, some recipes for the Champagne Cocktail called for the addition of brandy or cognac for a stronger kick and bigger body. But no matter what goes into it, the Champagne Cocktail has always been the choice of prominent and well-heeled U.S. citizens because champagne commands a lofty price and is a status symbol in America.*

We at Employees Only choose to make this cocktail with Curaçao, specifically Grand Marnier. We find that it adds more flavor notes and blends more effortlessly than does cognac. It's a misconception that one must use the finest champagne in this cocktail. Please do not destroy a masterful tête de cuvee *with bitters and sugar. Use a well-rounded nonvintage brut, which has the bones for such a cocktail.*   MAKES 1 DRINK

½ ounce Grand Marnier

5 ounces brut champagne, chilled

1 raw brown sugar cube

4 or 5 dashes Angostura bitters

1 lemon twist

Pour the Grand Marnier into a champagne flute and slowly top it off with the chilled champagne. Place the sugar cube on a bar spoon and saturate it with the bitters. Carefully drop the cube into the flute. Twist the lemon peel over the drink, then discard.

LONG DRINKS AND FANCY COCKTAILS

LONG DRINKS AND FANCY COCKTAILS are actually two drink categories that we at Employees Only combine into one. Both categories are classic and hearken back to the time when consumption of mixed drinks enjoyed more liberty and was not viewed with prejudice and ignorance about its place in the overall gastronomical experience. These drinks actually date back to around the early 1920s, when bartenders started leaving the aperitif territory and venturing into a realm formerly reserved solely for wine.

A *long drink* is the classic reference to any drink containing between 5 and 9 ounces of liquid. Typically, a long drink will have lots of ice and mixer, perfect for warmer days. A long drink should be a perfect food companion and also must be balanced in such a way that it can be enjoyed by itself alone. Examples are Collinses, Fizzes, and Rickeys. The same criteria apply to fancy cocktails—Sours, Gimlets, Smashes, Margaritas, Cobblers, and their variations. The difference is that fancy cocktails are mainly served straight up in a cocktail glass.

At Employees Only, we take a classic approach to long drinks and fancy cocktails. This means we're inspired by old recipes and formulas, which we update to fit the modern palate. This is the realm where we experiment with flavors the most and test out new ingredients and techniques. These cocktails are the most dynamic and exciting in our repertoire. We share with you the fruits of cocktail-making efforts stretching back to the earliest bartenders. This legacy is yours to share and develop as you please.

AMELIA

We use the Amelia to transition the Cosmo drinkers into our dangerous world of subtle flavors. We chose vodka as the base spirit to showcase St-Germain without muddying its flavor. The Amelia is named in honor of an older Greek woman who gave Jason food and lodging when he ran out of money while traveling through Greece.
MAKES 1 DRINK

1¾ ounces Luksusowa potato vodka

1 ounce St-Germain elderflower liqueur

¾ ounce Boiron blackberry purée (or make your own; see below)

¾ ounce freshly squeezed lemon juice

1 mint sprig, for garnish

Pour the vodka, liqueur, purée, and juice into a mixing glass. Add large cold ice cubes and shake vigorously. Strain into a chilled cocktail glass. Place the mint sprig in the palm of your hand and smack it with your other hand to release the aroma. Gently place the mint on the surface of the cocktail and serve.

BLACKBERRY PURÉE

¼ pound fresh or frozen, thawed blackberries (about 1 cup)

2 tablespoons superfine sugar

2 tablespoons water

2 tablespoons freshly squeezed lemon juice

Combine all ingredients in a blender. Liquefy and strain through a coarse sieve. Refrigerate until use. Will keep for 3 to 4 days, refrigerated.   MAKES ABOUT 1 CUP

DOMINANT FLAVORS: blackberries with mint on the nose
BODY: full-textured from the blackberries
DRYNESS: medium to dry
COMPLEXITY: medium complexity between blackberries and elderflower

ACCENTUATING OR CONTRASTING FLAVORS: contrasting elderflower with aroma of fresh mint
FINISH: short, dry with citrus overtones

GLASS: cocktail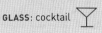

Tasting Notes

COSMOPOLITAN

By the time Sex in the City *featured Carrie and the Cosmo, we were already killing this contemporary cocktail during our tenure at Pravda in the late 1990s. Our recipe stood out in the world of popular downtown nightlife destinations as the hallmark of what a Cosmopolitan should be; light pink and citrusy, with ice shards and foam surrounding a flamed orange peel. Although it speaks to trendy fashionistas, when made properly the Cosmopolitan can be a tasty libation. Clubs and marketing agencies later bastardized this drink with Rose's lime juice, cheap triple sec, and enough cranberry juice to cure a bladder infection.*   MAKES 1 DRINK

1½ ounces Charbay Meyer lemon vodka

1 ounce Cointreau

¾ ounce freshly squeezed lime juice

1 ounce cranberry juice

1 orange twist, for garnish

Pour the vodka, Cointreau, and juices into a mixing glass. Add large cold ice cubes and shake vigorously. Strain into a chilled cocktail glass. Garnish with the orange twist.

Tasting Notes

DOMINANT FLAVORS: heavy citrus blast of lemon, lime, and orange

BODY: medium, crisp

DRYNESS: dry to medium

COMPLEXITY: low, one dimensional

ACCENTUATING OR CONTRASTING FLAVORS: cranberry adds slight tannins against citrus

FINISH: long, dry, acid with slight bitter orange overtones

GLASS: cocktail

AVIATION

The return of the Aviation cocktail signaled the rebirth of the classic cocktail. Using ingredients that were obscure a mere ten years ago, this drink is simple and snappy and speaks of the era surrounding Prohibition. The original Aviation cocktail was created in the early years of the twentieth century by one of us—a New York bartender, Hugo Ensslin, who was the head bartender at the Wallick Hotel. Probably his intention was to celebrate the Wright Brothers and other achievements in flight made at that time. Ensslin also published the recipe in his book, Recipes for Mixed Drinks, *which appeared in 1916 and in which he called for dry gin, lemon juice, maraschino, and crème de violette. We must assume that the crème de violette Ensslin had at his disposal is different than the ones we have today, as the drink does not turn sky-blue. Harry Craddock left out the crème de violette in* The Savoy Cocktail Book *and so did many others. Only recently have we begun to see the emergence of really high-quality crème de violette on the market—but it still remains to be seen if it will catch on beyond cocktail geekery. We add a touch of aromatic bitters at the end to dazzle your nose and create depth.*

MAKES 1 DRINK

1½ ounces Plymouth gin

1 ounce freshly squeezed lemon juice

¾ ounce Luxardo maraschino liqueur

¼ ounce simple syrup (page 154)

1 dash Angostura bitters

1 lemon wheel, for garnish

1 brandied cherry (see page 36), for garnish

Pour the gin, juice, liqueur, and syrup into a mixing glass. Add large cold ice cubes and shake vigorously. Strain into a chilled cocktail glass. Add the bitters and garnish with the lemon wheel and cherry.

DOMINANT FLAVORS: juniper and citrus
BODY: light, crisp citrus-driven
DRYNESS: medium to dry
COMPLEXITY: medium

ACCENTUATING OR CONTRASTING FLAVORS: maraschino cherry
FINISH: medium, lingering with maraschino overtones

GLASS: cocktail

Tasting Notes

BILLIONAIRE COCKTAIL

This cocktail was created in a flash of inspiration to showcase overproof whiskey by offsetting it with wonderfully lush and flavorful ingredients. Strong Baker's 107-proof bourbon serves as the backbone to the cocktail, providing vigor and heat. This is balanced with our rich homemade grenadine and fresh lemon juice to give a delightful sweet-and-sour balance. The Absinthe Bitters' anise essence rounds out the cocktail, giving it a classic feel and third dimension. After conceiving the recipe, we were stumped for a name until we realized it was quite similar to a version of the Prohibition classic Millionaire Cocktail (page 66). Because of inflation and the fact that ours is a "richer" cocktail, we named it the Billionaire Cocktail. MAKES 1 DRINK

2 ounces Baker's 107-proof bourbon

1 ounce freshly squeezed lemon juice

½ ounce simple syrup (page 154)

½ ounce homemade Grenadine (page 157)

¼ ounce Absinthe Bitters (page 161)

1 lemon wheel, for garnish

Pour the bourbon, juice, syrup, grenadine, and bitters into a mixing glass. Add large cold ice cubes and shake vigorously for 8 to 10 seconds. Strain into a chilled cocktail glass and garnish with the lemon wheel.

Tasting Notes

DOMINANT FLAVORS: whiskey forward, with pomegranate molasses

BODY: crisp, medium to full due to high proof whiskey

DRYNESS: medium

COMPLEXITY: high, rich flavors

ACCENTUATING OR CONTRASTING FLAVORS: Absinthe Bitters contrast pomegranate and whiskey

FINISH: long with lingering tannins and pomegranate overtones

GLASS: cocktail

MILLIONAIRE COCKTAIL

The Millionaire Cocktail is not as romanticized as the South Side or as revered as a Whiskey Sour. Little is known about this Prohibition-era cocktail except that it was a popular name for cocktails of that time. We have found five different cocktails carrying the moniker, with recipes varying from whiskey to rum to gin. Even Harry Craddock, author of The Savoy Cocktail Book, *listed two completely unrelated recipes as Millionaire Cocktail No. 1 and Millionaire Cocktail No. 2. The first consists of Jamaican rum, apricot brandy, sloe gin, lime juice, and grenadine; the second has anisette, egg white, gin, and absinthe. We have provided the Millionaire recipe from* The How and When *cocktail book by Hyman Gale and Gerald F. Marco, first printed in 1938. Although it inspired the name for our Billionaire Cocktail (page 64), we have made some slight adjustments to the proportions and added lemon juice for balance.* MAKES 1 DRINK

2 ounces Knob Creek bourbon

¾ ounce Grand Marnier

1 egg white

½ ounce homemade Grenadine (page 157)

¼ ounce Ricard pastis

½ ounce freshly squeezed lemon juice

Freshly grated nutmeg, for garnish

Pour the bourbon, liqueur, egg white, grenadine, pastis, and juice into a mixing glass. Add large cold ice cubes and shake vigorously. Strain into a chilled cocktail glass and garnish with the nutmeg.

Tasting Notes		
DOMINANT FLAVORS: whiskey forward with candied fruit flavors		**ACCENTUATING OR CONTRASTING FLAVORS:** nutmeg and anise flavors against whiskey
BODY: medium, creamy texture due to egg white		**FINISH:** medium
DRYNESS: medium		
COMPLEXITY: high		**GLASS:** cocktail 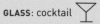

FRAISE SAUVAGE

The Fraise Sauvage was inspired by the famous pre-Prohibition classic, the French 75 (page 70). The name itself is a play on words in French, meaning "wild strawberry." This cocktail uses our EO homemade Wild Strawberry Cordial to create a cocktail in the classic style. We shake together Plymouth gin with fresh lemon juice, simple syrup, and strawberry cordial, then top it off with demi-sec champagne. For our first summer menu at Employees Only, we wanted to put on the list a cocktail that would be a crowd-pleaser. Fraise Sauvage is the EO equivalent of the ubiquitous Caprese salad. The flavors of gin, strawberry, and champagne are a timeless combination and showcase how simple flavors can become complex when combined. To make this cocktail without the strawberry cordial, simply muddle a whole fresh strawberry, then follow the rest of the directions. MAKES 1 DRINK

1¼ ounces Plymouth gin

½ ounce freshly squeezed lemon juice

¼ ounce simple syrup (page 154)

½ ounce Wild Strawberry Cordial (page 158)

2 ounces demi-sec champagne

1 half strawberry, for garnish

Pour the gin, juice, syrup, and cordial into a mixing glass. Add large cold ice cubes, cover, and shake vigorously for 7 or 8 seconds. Pour the champagne into a chilled cocktail glass and pour the cocktail over it. Garnish with half a strawberry.

DOMINANT FLAVORS: straightforward strawberry
BODY: light, crisp, full mouth of fruit
DRYNESS: medium
COMPLEXITY: low

ACCENTUATING OR CONTRASTING FLAVORS: hints of vanilla and juniper rounding to strawberry flavor
FINISH: medium with vanilla overtones

GLASS: cocktail

Tasting Notes

FRENCH 75

The name "French 75" refers to the most deadly and accurate artillery piece of World War I: the 75-mm field gun. Some credit WWI French-American flying ace Raoul Lufbery as the creator, who poured a little cognac into his beloved champagne for added kick. Other recipes list gin as the main ingredient in what is basically a Tom Collins with champagne instead of club soda. This recipe is first seen in The Savoy Cocktail Book; *author Harry Craddock notes that it "hits with remarkable precision." Across the pond, the French 75 was made popular at New York's infamous Stork Club, which opened during Prohibition and survived into the 1960s. Looking back at the historical cocktail record, it seems most likely that this cocktail began as the gin version, then makers shifted to cognac in order to make the drink a bit more French.* MAKES 1 DRINK

1¼ ounces Tanqueray No. 10 gin

½ ounce freshly squeezed lemon juice

¾ ounce simple syrup (page 154)

3 ounces Perrier-Jouët Grand Brut champagne

1 orange half-wheel, for garnish

Pour the gin, juice, and syrup into a mixing glass. Add large cold ice cubes and shake vigorously. Pour the champagne into a large wine goblet over large cold ice cubes and drop in the orange half-wheel. Strain the cocktail over it.

The story of the Roselle highlights the creative process at Employees Only. After seeking a hibiscus cordial, bar manager Robert Krueger infused the dried blossoms into syrup for a delicious result. The citrus and floral elements immediately suggested a pairing with gin, and the botanicals in Tanqueray No. 10 specifically led to grapefruit. A quick shake revealed that the red of the hibiscus turns an iridescent rose when mixed—inspiring the drink's name. The resulting drink is a reminder that a confident bartender should never be afraid of mixing a pink drink—or of drinking one, for that matter. MAKES 1 DRINK

> 1½ ounces Tanqueray No. 10 gin
>
> 1 ounce Hibiscus Cordial (page 158)
>
> ¾ ounce freshly squeezed lime juice
>
> ½ ounce freshly squeezed grapefruit juice

Pour the gin, cordial, and juices into a mixing glass. Add large cold ice cubes and shake vigorously. Strain into a chilled cocktail glass.

DOMINANT FLAVORS: floral hibiscus and grapefruit
BODY: medium
DRYNESS: medium
COMPLEXITY: low to medium

ACCENTUATING OR CONTRASTING FLAVORS: citrus and juniper
FINISH: medium tannic hibiscus with juniper following

GLASS: cocktail

Tasting Notes

GIMLET

The Gimlet, invented by a medical doctor, was born out of necessity. Sir Thomas D. Gimlette, a British naval surgeon, prescribed his vitamin-packed cocktail to sailors to prevent scurvy. His daily dose consisted of navy-strength Plymouth gin, which was rationed to officers (common sailors drank rum), and lime cordial, which was a way of preserving lime juice on long sea voyages. The Gimlet found its way into social drinking and became as recognized as the Martini or Manhattan, due to the instant availability of Rose's Lime Juice. Unfortunately, over years of de-evolution, lime cordials on the market fell victim to the same pressures as other mass-produced products—to become more profitable. Today, most have little to do with lime and more to do with high-fructose corn syrup and artificial colorings. With the rebirth of the classic cocktail over the last decade, many enthusiasts have decided that fresh lime juice and simple syrup are the way to go, but in our opinion, the resulting "gin daiquiri" does not honor the spirit of the original cocktail and should not be called a Gimlet. True Gimlet drinkers look down their noses at such an abomination. To bridge the gap between both camps, we created our own all-natural lime cordial using lime and kaffir lime leaf. It is stunningly simple and classically structured but surprisingly novel and sophisticated.   MAKES 1 DRINK

> 2 ounces Plymouth gin
> ¾ ounce homemade Lime Cordial (page 157)
> 1 lime wheel, for garnish

Pour the gin and cordial into a mixing glass. Add large cold ice cubes and shake briefly but with conviction. Strain into a rocks glass over large cold ice cubes and garnish with a lime wheel.

Tasting Notes

DOMINANT FLAVORS: juniper and lime
BODY: medium with sweet-sour tongue coating
DRYNESS: dry to medium
COMPLEXITY: medium

ACCENTUATING OR CONTRASTING FLAVORS: hints of kaffir lime oils with honeyed agave
FINISH: long, lingering, gasping-for-air finish

GLASS: rocks

LEFT TO RIGHT: Gin Rickey (page 75), Gimlet, Grapefruit Gimlet (page 74)

GRAPEFRUIT GIMLET

The Grapefruit Gimlet (see photo on page 73) came as an inspiration upon tasting Charbay ruby red grapefruit vodka. Unlike other flavored vodkas, this producer actually uses real fruit in a natural process of infusion. Charbay pays Texas ruby red grapefruit growers premium prices to leave the fruit on the tree until they are overripe. Then they are shipped to California, where father-and-son distillers Miles and Marko Karakasevic grind the whole fruits—skins, pulp, and juice—then let them sit in alcohol for six months to extract the real fruit flavor. This essence is then strained and added to clear vodka. The result of this infusion is unlike any other flavored vodka. The beauty of our Grapefruit Gimlet is that it consists of only three ingredients: Charbay grapefruit vodka, fresh lime juice, and agave nectar. This recipe is very simple to make and really accentuates the grapefruit vodka. Make it and taste it and you'll feel like you've just bitten into a sweet, ripe ruby red grapefruit through the skin. It's refreshing and full flavored, and it begs for another sip. MAKES 1 DRINK

2 ounces Charbay ruby red grapefruit vodka

1 ounce freshly squeezed lime juice

¾ ounce agave nectar

1 ruby red grapefruit quarter-wheel, for garnish

Pour the vodka, juice, and nectar into a mixing glass. Add large cold ice cubes and shake vigorously for a few seconds. Strain into a rocks glass over large cold ice cubes and garnish with the grapefruit wheel.

Tasting Notes

DOMINANT FLAVORS: full mouth of grapefruit
BODY: medium, like biting into a grapefruit rind
DRYNESS: dry to medium
COMPLEXITY: low, straightforward flavor

ACCENTUATING OR CONTRASTING FLAVORS: honeyed agave
FINISH: medium, with grapefruit oil overtones

GLASS: rocks

The Gin Rickey (see photo on page 73) is the most prominent member of the Rickey Cocktail family, which basically calls for a shot of any straight spirit, a splash of freshly squeezed lime juice, and club soda, served tall. The story has it that the founding father of this cocktail trend was a retired Civil War colonel and lobbyist, Joe Rickey. The man loved his bourbon with soda and a squeeze of lime. He refused sugar on the grounds that "drinks with sugar heat the blood," and as a string-puller in D.C., he clearly didn't want passion to interfere with clear thinking. We played with this cocktail but shelved it, feeling that although it is a wonderful drink, it was not intriguing enough to put on our menu. Then we made our own lime cordial. The concentrated flavor of the sweetened cordial created the same feel as the original, only with more depth and intensity and more focus on the gin. Also, our lime cordial is sweetened not with sugar but with agave nectar, which has a much lower glycemic index and therefore should not "heat" the blood as much. The good colonel would be pleased. MAKES 1 DRINK

1¾ ounces Plymouth gin

¾ ounce homemade Lime Cordial (page 157)

4 ounces club soda

1 lime wheel, for garnish

In a tall Collins glass, build the drink by pouring in the gin and lime cordial. Fill up with large cold ice cubes and cover the glass with a small shaker top. Shake briefly, remove the shaker top, and top off with the club soda. Garnish with the lime wheel.

DOMINANT FLAVORS: juniper and lime
BODY: light, refreshing
DRYNESS: dry to medium
COMPLEXITY: low

ACCENTUATING OR CONTRASTING FLAVORS: kaffir lime oils and honeyed agave
FINISH: short, carbonated

GLASS: Collins

Tasting Notes

The original Gin Julep published in Harry Johnson's 1882 Bartenders' Manual *was the only other julep that people generally ordered besides the whiskey and brandy versions. It's likely that the prominent malt flavor of Holland gin, a product we know today as genever, appealed to the whiskey lover. With the rerelease of Bols Genever gin to the U.S. marketplace, we tested this cocktail but were not at first happy with the results. So we cut the amount of genever in half and substituted Plymouth gin for the other half—and then we had one of those great drinks that will stand the test of time. It is unlike most cocktails because it has two base spirits. It is delicate, light yet full-flavored, and very refreshing. It is a cocktail to fall in love with.* MAKES 1 DRINK

15 large mint leaves

½ ounce homemade Mint Syrup (page 156)

1 ounce Bols Genever gin

1 ounce Plymouth gin

1 splash club soda

1 mint sprig, for garnish

Muddle the mint leaves and mint syrup in the bottom of a rocks or Old Fashioned glass. Fill the glass with large cold ice cubes. Pour in the genever and Plymouth gin. Add the club soda. Garnish with the mint sprig.

DOMINANT FLAVORS: strong fresh mint
BODY: medium to high
DRYNESS: off-dry
COMPLEXITY: high, subtle complexity

ACCENTUATING OR CONTRASTING FLAVORS: malt and juniper round the base
FINISH: sweet with lingering mint overtones

GLASS: rocks

Tasting Notes

MINT JULEP

This Mint Julep is the quintessential American cocktail, so regal that it sits at the summit of cocktail Olympus next to classics like the Martini, the Manhattan, and the Sazerac. It hails from Kentucky and Virginia and is enjoyed throughout the South. We know for sure it was consumed as early as 1790, particularly in the summertime. A particular type of spearmint, Kentucky Colonel, is best suited for the preparation of this cocktail, commonly served in a silver or pewter cup to keep it chilled longer. Since 1938, it has been the official drink of the Kentucky Derby, where up to 120,000 mint juleps are served over the period of two days.

There are many historical and regional versions: some use bourbon, others brandy; some only tap the mint, others pulverize it into a paste. We favor a bourbon recipe in which fresh spearmint is bruised with a ladle, then sugar, bitters, and bourbon are added; the mixture is chilled overnight so the mint releases all the flavors and essential oils into the whiskey, then strained the following day for final julep preparation. To simplify this process so the julep can be made to order, we use our own homemade Mint Syrup. MAKES 1 DRINK

3-finger pinch fresh spearmint leaves

½ ounce homemade Mint Syrup (page 156)
or ½ ounce simple syrup (page 154)

2 dashes Angostura bitters

1 splash sparkling water or club soda

2 ounces Maker's Mark bourbon

1 mint sprig, for garnish

Muddle the spearmint leaves with the Mint Syrup and bitters in the bottom of a rocks or Old Fashioned glass. Add the sparkling water. Fill the glass with crushed ice and add the bourbon. Gently stir and garnish with the mint sprig.

Tasting Notes

DOMINANT FLAVORS: mint and caramel
BODY: medium
DRYNESS: medium
COMPLEXITY: medium

ACCENTUATING OR CONTRASTING FLAVORS: sweet oak coming out of the cold ice
FINISH: short, sharp, fresh

GLASS: rocks

HAVANA-STYLE MOJITO

The Mojito was born at the La Bodeguita del Medio in Havana, Cuba, in the 1940s. Legend has it that Ernest Hemingway wrote "My Mojito in La Bodeguita," which still can be read today, hanging on the wall. Others claim that this was a forgery, a marketing ploy of the restaurant owners to promote their mojito cocktail and bring in tourists after communism took over. Over the last decade, the Mojito has quietly become one of the most recognized drinks in the world. Today, people carelessly consume it regardless of the season or weather. But somewhere along the way, the mojito has been reconfigured as a short, stout, bittersweet rum hybrid of muddled lime wedges and pulverized mint. Then a friend of ours who went to film school in Cuba came back and pointed out that mojitos were supposed to be tall, light, and fizzy, clean and effervescent. We brought it back to its true form and labeled it the Havana-Style Mojito. Although it never made it onto our menu, it is the closest you can get to a true mojito without the luxury of Havana Club Cuban rum. It is a fantastic cocktail—but please don't order it while there is snow on the ground. MAKES 1 DRINK

3 pinches fresh mint leaves

1½ teaspoons superfine sugar

½ ounce homemade Mint Syrup (page 156)

1¼ ounces freshly squeezed lime juice

1¾ ounces Flor de Caña four-year-old rum

1 ounce club soda

2 dashes Angostura bitters, for garnish

Lightly muddle the mint leaves with the sugar in the bottom of a Collins glass. Add the syrup, juice, and rum. Fill with large cold ice cubes and shake briefly. Top off with the club soda. Garnish with the bitters.

DOMINANT FLAVORS: mint and lime
BODY: light, sparkling
DRYNESS: medium
COMPLEXITY: medium to low, depending on the rum

ACCENTUATING OR CONTRASTING FLAVORS: grass and molasses
FINISH: short, fresh

GLASS: Collins

Tasting Notes

LEFT TO RIGHT:

Ginger Smash, Spring Season (page 83)

Ginger Smash, Summer Season (page 84)

Ginger Smash, Winter Season (page 82)

Ginger Smash, Fall Season (page 85)

GINGER SMASH

When we were composing the menu for Employees Only back in fall of 2004, we were building the restaurant mostly by ourselves and couldn't really afford any time away from the construction site. So we had just one afternoon to test our recipes before opening. Although we had discussed ideas beforehand and were clear on the direction of the opening menu, and had even created infusions and ingredients on our own time, we'd not had the chance to create the cocktails we had envisioned. But it all worked seamlessly in one afternoon in our "laboratory" in Williamsburg, Brooklyn.

The one cocktail that came out unexpectedly was the Ginger Smash. The term "smash" refers to an old family of drinks, similar to juleps, in which mint would be muddled into

spirits of any kind. Ginger has always been a favorite "hot" ingredient of ours, but when we combined fresh cranberries and gingerroot, muddled with sugar, the result was unlike anything we had tasted or made before. Short, snappy, tart, fresh cranberries; the heat from the ginger and gin; sweet apple cordial from Germany; and a little lemon juice produced the most complex ginger cocktail we had ever witnessed. After our December opening, it ranked as our number two selling cocktail. In February, with fresh cranberries out of season, we tried frozen, but they had no snap. This forced us to create a Ginger Smash for each season, using the spirit and fruit accompaniment dictated by the current harvest. All showcase ginger and are smashed or muddled.

GINGER SMASH, WINTER SEASON

This version of the Ginger Smash is the original Employees Only seasonal cocktail. We set out to create a cocktail composed of ingredients that warm you up on a winter day. The result was so tasty and fresh in aroma that it was a "smash" from the start. It remains, to this day, one of our best sellers. MAKES 1 DRINK

2 thin slices fresh gingerroot

10 fresh whole cranberries

1½ teaspoons superfine sugar

1½ ounces Plymouth gin

1½ ounces Berentzen Apfelkorn apple liqueur

¾ ounce freshly squeezed lemon juice

Muddle the ginger, cranberries, and sugar in the bottom of a mixing glass. Pour in the gin, apple liqueur, and juice and add enough large cold ice cubes to fill a rocks glass. Cover and shake hard but briefly. Pour unstrained into a rocks glass and serve.

Tasting Notes

DOMINANT FLAVORS: ginger and crisp apples
BODY: full, chewy, rich texture
DRYNESS: medium
COMPLEXITY: high

ACCENTUATING OR CONTRASTING FLAVORS: juniper and tart cranberries
FINISH: long, spicy with ginger overtones

GLASS: rocks

GINGER SMASH, SPRING SEASON

This version of the Ginger Smash was the last seasonal version added to our menu. When it was being created, we had become enamored with tequila and wanted to showcase it in the springtime. Pairing ginger with kumquats—small citrus fruits that come to market at the end of winter—we found the perfect canvas for 100-percent blue agave tequila. Its texture, slight velvety sweetness, and spiciness from fresh gingerroot make this drink one of our new favorites. MAKES 1 DRINK

2 thin slices fresh gingerroot

2 fresh whole kumquats

1 teaspoon superfine sugar

1½ ounces Partida Blanco tequila

1 ounce Rhum Clémente Créole Shrubb

¾ ounce freshly squeezed lime juice

Muddle the ginger, kumquats, and sugar in the bottom of a mixing glass. Add the tequila, Shrubb, and juice and enough large cold ice cubes to fill a rocks glass. Cover and shake hard but briefly. Pour unstrained into a rocks glass and serve.

DOMINANT FLAVORS: ginger and bitter oranges
BODY: full, velvety
DRYNESS: medium
COMPLEXITY: high, due to bitters

ACCENTUATING OR CONTRASTING FLAVORS: floral overtones of agave and tartness of kumquat oils
FINISH: long, spicy with citrus overtones

GLASS: rocks

Tasting Notes

GINGER SMASH, SUMMER SEASON

We had just finished working with the team that developed 10 Cane rum and wanted to use this excellent grassy pot-stilled spirit in a cocktail. Naturally, we gravitated toward fresh, sweet, and tangy pineapples, which are so common in the Caribbean. We added maraschino to the mix to help give a fruit punch to the more vegetal ingredients. The result is a cocktail so tropical and multidimensional that it will make your head spin, so tasty and good looking that you will fall in love with it instantly. MAKES 1 DRINK

2 thin slices fresh gingerroot

2 (1-inch) cubes fresh pineapple

1 teaspoon superfine sugar

1½ ounces 10 Cane rum

½ ounce freshly squeezed lime juice

½ ounce Maraska maraschino liqueur

½ ounce Berentzen Apfelkorn apple liqueur

1 pineapple leaf, for garnish

Muddle the ginger, pineapple, and sugar in the bottom of a mixing glass. Pour in the rum, lime juice, and maraschino and apple liqueurs. Add large cold ice cubes and shake vigorously. Pour unstrained into a rocks glass. Garnish with the pineapple leaf.

Tasting Notes

DOMINANT FLAVORS: pineapple and ginger
BODY: full, rich-textured
DRYNESS: medium
COMPLEXITY: high

ACCENTUATING OR CONTRASTING FLAVORS: grassiness from the rum and gaminess from the maraschino
FINISH: long, spicy, fruity

GLASS: rocks

GINGER SMASH, FALL SEASON

This fall version of the Ginger Smash has been with us for years, but it truly came together with the addition of allspice dram, a highly bitter and aromatized liqueur. It contrasts two of our favorite ingredients—pears and ginger. Gin mixes very well with pears because it helps open up the subtle aromas that these pome fruits are prized for. Green Bartlett pears are our choice in this cocktail because of their tartness and solid nature. Feel free to try whatever pear you can find in its peak of season. MAKES 1 DRINK

2 thin slices fresh gingerroot

5 thin slices Bartlett pear

1 teaspoon superfine sugar

1½ ounces Plymouth gin

1½ ounces Berentzen Apfelkorn apple liqueur

¾ ounce freshly squeezed lemon juice

1 dash St. Elizabeth allspice dram

Muddle the ginger, pear, and sugar in the bottom of a mixing glass. Add the gin, apple liqueur, juice, and allspice dram and add enough large cold ice cubes to fill a rocks glass. Cover and shake hard but briefly. Pour unstrained into a rocks glass and serve.

DOMINANT FLAVORS: pears and ginger
BODY: full-textured, with soft fruits
DRYNESS: medium
COMPLEXITY: medium

ACCENTUATING OR CONTRASTING FLAVORS: juniper, allspice, and crisp apples round out the pears
FINISH: short, crisp, warm ginger

GLASS: rocks

Tasting Notes

WHISKEY SMASH

According to David Wondrich, the Whiskey Smash comes from the Baroque Age (see opposite page) of the cocktail. Obviously, it served as inspiration for our seasonal Ginger Smash cocktails, but it is in all its features a julep—the only difference being that the Smash has some ornamental fruits for garnish and is always shaken so that the mint is "smashed"—hence the name. From all the smashes in the Baroque Age, it appears that the Brandy Smash was the most popular (same drink, different base spirit—try it out for yourself), but somehow the whiskey version stuck with us. Maybe sampling Dale DeGroff's rocking peach whiskey smash sealed the deal for us, or maybe it was just that we loved the term "smashed." In any case, this is a very simple drink to make, and we suggest that you use our homemade Mint Syrup in place of simple syrup for a far more dimensional cocktail experience. This cocktail is one of the very few that contains no juice but nevertheless should be shaken and smashed. MAKES 1 DRINK

2 orange half-wheels

1-finger pinch fresh mint leaves

½ ounce homemade Mint Syrup (page 156)

2 ounces Michter's US No.1 Rye Whiskey

Seasonal berries (strawberries, blackberries, blueberries, raspberries, currants, black currants, mulberries), for garnish

1 mint sprig, for garnish

Fill a rocks or Old Fashioned glass with shaved ice and put the orange half-wheels inside so that they cover the walls of the glass. In the bottom of a mixing glass, gently tap the mint leaves to release their essence and macerate them with the Mint Syrup. Add the whiskey and large cold ice cubes. Shake vigorously and strain into the prepared glass. Garnish with the berries and mint sprig.

Tasting Notes

DOMINANT FLAVORS: mint and whiskey
BODY: light, coarse, wet mouthfeel
DRYNESS: medium
COMPLEXITY: low

ACCENTUATING OR CONTRASTING FLAVORS: it's all mint versus whiskey
FINISH: short, sweet

GLASS: rocks

THE ERAS OF THE COCKTAIL

The Archaic Age (1783–1830)

The primordial cocktails. Punches and blending occurs. Mostly regional drinks. Recipes come together without tools or techniques.

The Golden Age of the Cocktail: The Baroque and Classic Ages

THE BAROQUE AGE (1830–1885)

The foundations of mixology are laid. Tools are incorporated. Recipes are categorized. Commercially available ice comes onto the scene. Technique is established.

THE CLASSIC AGE (1885–1920)

Cocktails with juices, egg whites, and syrups gain in popularity. The shake becomes the signature technique in drink making. Many of the classics are created during this era.

The Dark Age (Prohibition, 1920–1933)

In the United States, cocktail bartenders go underground or out of the country. Drinks in the United States suffer from a lack of quality ingredients. New ways are found to mask bad hooch.

The Deco Age (1920–1939)

New cocktails come out of the Caribbean and Europe. In the post-Prohibition states, cocktails made popular in speakeasies are standardized.

The Industrialized Food Age (1945–1965)

Factory farming takes hold in America. Fresh is replaced with manufactured. Tiki drinks become popular. The Martini becomes a cocktail icon. Bartenders turn to liqueurs as flavor enhancers.

The Second Dark Age (1966–1990)

Counterculture leads young people to other forms of recreational intoxications. Drinking culture is dictated by billboards. Marketing agencies push cocktails that make drink making easier and skill-less. Highballs rule this era. Disco and "shot" drinks become popular.

The Renaissance (1991–2009)

Premium and craft spirits appear in the marketplace. Classic tools and methodology reemerge. The Martini craze paves the way for new ingredients in cocktail making. Proper cocktail-driven bars emerge.

The Platinum Age (Present)

Classic and crafted cocktails have never been more popular worldwide. Many restaurants include a cocktail list in their beverage programs. Sommeliers and chefs see the importance of the cocktail as part of the gastronomical experience.

GRAND FASHIONED

This *Grand Fashioned was the first-place winner of Grand Marnier and the New York Film Festival's Independent Cocktail Festival in 1999, long before we ever opened Employees Only. The idea was to get two ounces of Grand Marnier into a cocktail without being cloyingly sweet. To balance this much Curaçao, we muddle fresh blood oranges with lime juice, sugar, and dashes of Angostura bitters. This cocktail looked so much like the contemporary recipe for an Old Fashioned that the name just took over. For the competition, we garnished the drink with a kumquat that had to be tediously scored and peeled to resemble a "blossom," then stained inside with grenadine. You can imagine our surprise when, upon winning, we were told we would need to make five hundred of these cocktails at the premiere for* All About My Mother *by director Pedro Almodóvar. The Grand Fashioned is so rich and luscious that it can be consumed as an after-dinner drink.*   MAKES 1 DRINK

1 teaspoon superfine sugar

3 dashes Angostura bitters

3 blood orange wedges, peeled

2 ounces Grand Marnier

¾ ounce freshly squeezed lime juice

Muddle the sugar, bitters, and oranges in the bottom of a mixing glass. Add the Grand Marnier and juice. Add enough large cold ice cubes to fit in a rocks glass and shake hard but briefly. Pour all the unstrained liquid into a rocks glass and serve.

Tasting Notes

DOMINANT FLAVORS: blood oranges
BODY: full, rich-textured
DRYNESS: sweet
COMPLEXITY: medium to high

ACCENTUATING OR CONTRASTING FLAVORS: bitters add depth and richness
FINISH: medium with blood orange overtones

GLASS: rocks

OLD FASHIONED #1

The name "Old Fashioned" here refers to what was once known as the Whiskey Cocktail. It is a cocktail in the simplest terms: spirit, water, bitters, and sugar. Sometime in the late 1800s, the use of the word "cocktail" broadened far beyond its original definition, so it was necessary to come up with a new moniker to distinguish the older cousin. Many self-described purists will argue that there is only one way to make this drink properly. We disagree. So if you decide to order a whiskey cocktail as an Old Fashioned, be precise about what you want. Intentionally being ambiguous about your order is just a nice way of being obnoxious. MAKES 1 DRINK

1 raw brown sugar cube

2 dashes Angostura bitters

¼ ounce cold water

2 ounces American whiskey (at least 100-proof; rye, bourbon, corn, or blended)

1 lemon twist, for garnish

Muddle the sugar, bitters, and water in the bottom of a rocks glass. Add the whiskey and 1 large cold ice cube. Twist the lemon peel over the drink and drop it in.

DOMINANT FLAVORS: whiskey with lemon on the nose
BODY: full, high alcohol content
DRYNESS: dry
COMPLEXITY: low

ACCENTUATING OR CONTRASTING FLAVORS: bitters working with burnt sugar
FINISH: short with oak and citrus oil overtones

GLASS: rocks

Tasting Notes

OLD FASHIONED #2

We will not simply turn a blind eye to the contemporary version of the Old Fashioned—it was the first cocktail we were taught that used bitters. Somewhere between the 1890s and 1930s, what probably started out as an ornamental garnish of orange and cherry fell into the mixing glass and got muddled with sugar and bitters. We see evidence of this drink in Burke's Complete Cocktail and Drinking Recipes *from 1936, in which the fruit is muddled, whereas during the same period* Old Mr. Boston Bartender's Guide *continued to add the fruit after making the drink. More than likely it was a trick used during Prohibition to mask poor-quality booze that stuck with many and was passed down over the generations. Today, many look down on this version of the cocktail, mostly because of the use of commercial, artificial maraschino cherries. Many young cocktail enthusiasts may not have enjoyed this cocktail in its original form, so we offer this restoration for them.* MAKES 1 DRINK

1 raw brown sugar cube

½ teaspoon superfine sugar

3 dashes Angostura bitters

2 orange half-wheels

4 brandied cherries (see page 36)

2 lemon twists

2 splashes club soda

2½ ounces Rittenhouse 100-proof rye whiskey

Muddle the sugars, bitters, 1 orange half-wheel, 3 of the cherries, and 1 lemon twist in the bottom of a rocks glass. Discard the orange and lemon skins. Add a splash of the club soda. Fill up the glass with large cold ice cubes. Carefully pour the whiskey on top. Finish with another splash of club soda and garnish with the remaining orange half-wheel, brandied cherry, and lemon twist.

GREENWICH SOUR

Stunning to look at, the Greenwich Sour is rich and frothy, with a band of red wine floating on top. It is a variation of a Prohibition classic, the New York Sour. The key difference between the two is that we have added an egg white in our take, a practice common throughout the history of making sours. Many people today are wary about consuming raw eggs for fear of salmonella. The risk of contamination is actually quite low and can be reduced even more by using eggs from free-range chickens; add high-proof spirit to that, and the chances of getting sick are reduced to almost nothing. The egg white adds texture to the cocktail by trapping air and requires a very long hard shake to create the necessary consistency. Many bartenders will shake the egg white on its own first to begin this process. To give the Greenwich Sour its necessary backbone, it is important to use high-proof whiskey to cut through the sour body. The wine's tannins add depth to the cocktail and complete its finish. MAKES 1 DRINK

1¾ ounces Wild Turkey 101-proof rye whiskey

¾ ounce freshly squeezed lemon juice

¾ ounce simple syrup (page 154)

1 egg white

1 orange half-wheel, for garnish

1 brandied cherry (see page 36), for garnish

¾ ounce dry red wine (Malbec or Syrah)

Pour the whiskey, juice, syrup, and egg white into a mixing glass. Add large cold ice cubes and shake vigorously for at least 1 minute; when your hands start to freeze and you can't shake any more, you'll know it's enough. Strain into a rocks glass over large cold ice cubes. Float the red wine on top (see page 23). Garnish with the orange and cherry.

NEW YORK SOUR

We discovered the New York Sour in the summer of 2003 while we were researching cocktails to put on the opening drink list for Keith McNally's Schiller's Liquor Bar on the Lower East Side. Visually inviting, this sour is deep yellow with a crimson band of red wine floating on top. The origin of the cocktail is shrouded in mystery, but it is certain that it was served at several New York City speakeasies in the late 1920s. It was no surprise to discover that this cocktail was New York's Prohibition-era favorite, probably because the lemon juice, sugar, and wine camouflaged and successfully balanced the bad watered-down whiskey common in those days. It was the cool drink to have, and people who ordered it were "in the know." Think of it as the Prohibition-era Cosmo—or any other status-symbol cocktail that clearly advertises itself in appearance. Made with better ingredients, the cocktail became a masterpiece of complex flavors and mouthfeel. A chef friend of ours once remarked that this drink is like sangria à la minute—and one of the few cocktails that can be successfully paired with a main course.

MAKES 1 DRINK

1¾ ounces Rittenhouse 100-proof rye whiskey

¾ ounce freshly squeezed lemon juice

¾ ounce simple syrup (page 154)

¾ ounce dry red wine (Malbec or Syrah)

1 orange half-wheel, for garnish

1 brandied cherry (see page 36), for garnish

Pour the whiskey, juice, and syrup into a mixing glass. Add large cold ice cubes and shake vigorously. Strain over large cold new ice cubes into a rocks glass. Carefully float the wine on top (see page 23). Garnish with the orange and cherry.

Tasting Notes

DOMINANT FLAVORS: whiskey, citrus, and stone fruits
BODY: crisp, medium
DRYNESS: medium to dry, with crisp acidity
COMPLEXITY: medium

ACCENTUATING OR CONTRASTING FLAVORS: oak and wine tannins
FINISH: short crisp citrus followed by red wine tannins

GLASS: rocks

WHISKEY SOUR

The Whiskey Sour is the pinnacle of the sour cocktail family and unarguably its most famous member. In Harry Johnson's Bartenders' Manual, *the preferred method is to stir together sugar, water, and lemon juice before shaking with whiskey. During the dark ages of the cocktail in the 1970s and '80s, it was turned into a two-ingredient drink in which cheap blended whiskey was poured over ice with sweet-and-sour mix from a soda gun. However, the real Whiskey Sour has been resurrected and can be made in its pure form almost anywhere that has a decent cocktail menu, even by aspiring actors working as bartenders. It is a very straightforward cocktail with a strong base of whiskey mixed with simple syrup and sour, freshly squeezed lemon juice. To bring together the body, add a splash of orange juice—just realize that with more than a splash, this drink becomes a Stone Sour. It is a fairly easy drink that can help you master the balance between sweet and sour to spirit. Make sure you shake it enough so that a thin foam rests on the surface—that is the hallmark for Whiskey Sour fans.*

MAKES 1 DRINK

2 ounces Rittenhouse 100-proof rye whiskey

1 ounce freshly squeezed lemon juice

½ ounce freshly squeezed orange juice

¾ ounce simple syrup (page 154)

1 orange half-wheel, for garnish

1 brandied cherry (see page 36), for garnish

Pour the whiskey, juices, and syrup into a mixing glass. Add large cold ice cubes and shake vigorously. Strain into a chilled rocks or Old Fashioned glass over large cold ice cubes. Garnish with the orange and cherry.

Tasting Notes

DOMINANT FLAVORS: citrus and whiskey
BODY: clean, medium
DRYNESS: medium with crisp acidity
COMPLEXITY: low

ACCENTUATING OR CONTRASTING FLAVORS: orange, oak
FINISH: short, crisp, acidic

GLASS: rocks

There is an old tale about a creature that dwells in the Pine Barrens of southern New Jersey. The Jersey Devil is three and a half feet tall, with hoofed hind legs, claws on its front legs, a horse-like head, and bat wings. Rumored to be born of a witch and Satan himself, the Jersey Devil has been blamed for odd sightings, missing people, and stolen livestock since colonial days. Around the same time the legend was born, the Laird family began distilling apple cider. Perfecting the family recipe for applejack, the Laird & Company Distillery became the first commercial distillery in America and is still in business today. They even weathered Prohibition, selling sweet cider and applesauce until they received a special license to produce "medicinal brandy." Their two main products are Laird's Apple Brandy and Laird's AppleJack. The brandy is a 100-proof spirit distilled solely from apples; the AppleJack is a blended spirit of 35 percent apple brandy and 65 percent whiskey. Our Jersey Devil cocktail artistically uses the 100-percent apple brandy and blends it with a unique ingredient—the English Bishop, which calls for roasting a clove-studded orange in a fire and infusing it with port wine. This drink was one of the first to fall into our "fancy cocktail" category because of the detail in the ingredients. It's also a killer drink and can be successfully used to bait and tranquilize a Jersey Devil. MAKES 1 DRINK

1¾ ounces English Bishop (page 160)

1½ ounces Laird's straight apple brandy

½ ounce Berentzen Apfelkorn apple liqueur

3 dashes Peychaud's bitters

1 orange half-wheel, for garnish

Pour the English Bishop, brandy, apple liqueur, and bitters into a mixing glass. Add large cold ice cubes and stir for 40 revolutions. Strain into a chilled cocktail glass. Garnish with the orange wheel.

DOMINANT FLAVORS: mulled wine and brandy
BODY: silky, smooth texture
DRYNESS: off-dry
COMPLEXITY: very layered

ACCENTUATING OR CONTRASTING FLAVORS: cloves and apples
FINISH: lingering, spicy

GLASS: cocktail

Tasting Notes

JACK ROSE

Before corporate America overwhelmed New York City with its massive amounts of money, shallowness, and brainwashing, the Big Apple was a very lively and dangerous place. Historically, no other city housed such a menagerie of characters, lowlifes, gangsters, and crooks, whose activities gained them a healthy prominence and romantic fame. One of those guys was Jacob "Jack" Rosenzweig, aka Jack Rose. Born in Poland, this famous gambler of the day grew up in the late 1800s in Connecticut and later moved to New York City, where he opened a gambling den, Second Avenue. Although he was not of the caliber of Lucky Luciano or Meyer Lansky, he became very popular when he turned state's evidence against Lieutenant Charles Becker, a crooked cop linked to bookies and gambling houses around town. Due to Jack Rose's testimony, Becker was convicted and received the death sentence. Jack in turn became a hero for the common man. The Jack Rose cocktail was created in his honor in 1912 or 1913, using applejack as the dominant ingredient. It remained a crowd-pleaser throughout the Prohibition era because apple brandy was easy to bootleg and was considered one of the safest spirits of the day. We love the version with our homemade grenadine and believe that it makes a fantastic contribution to this Prohibition-era classic. MAKES 1 DRINK

1½ ounces Laird's straight apple brandy or AppleJack

¾ ounce freshly squeezed lemon juice

½ ounce simple syrup (page 154)

¼ ounce homemade Grenadine (page 157)

Pour all the ingredients into a mixing glass. Add large cold ice cubes and shake vigorously. Strain into a chilled cocktail glass.

Tasting Notes

DOMINANT FLAVORS: apple and lemon
BODY: crisp, light
DRYNESS: medium
COMPLEXITY: low

ACCENTUATING OR CONTRASTING FLAVORS: candied pomegranates
FINISH: medium, well-rounded

GLASS: cocktail

The Mai Tai cocktail is Elvis with a guitar singing in the sunset in Hawaii. It was invented in 1944 by Victor "Trader Vic" Bergeron, who mixed Jamaican rum, lime juice, a few dashes of orange Curaçao, French almond syrup, and rock candy syrup. According to Trader Vic history, it was served to some friends from Tahiti, who promptly proclaimed "Mai tai, roa ae!"—which in Tahitian means "Out of this world, the best!" When this drink is made right, it is really, really super tasty. By default this cocktail is in the Tiki cocktail family, which became popular after World War II when soldiers from the South Pacific returned home in the 1940s and '50s. This trend began in Hawaii and on the West Coast and, then traveled across the nation. Unfortunately, like most cocktails of that era, the recipe was artificialized and cheapened over several decades and even now in Hawaii it is still made with commercial Mai Tai mixers and artificial flavors. At Employees Only, we make our tribute to this Tiki classic with twelve-year-old Flor de Caña Nicaraguan rum, the best French orange Curaçao, Lebanese almond syrup, and fresh lime juice. The traditional rock candy syrup was left out to keep the cocktail balanced, not just sweet. MAKES 1 DRINK

1½ ounces Flor de Caña 12-year-old rum

¾ ounce Marie Brizard orange Curaçao

¾ ounce orgeat or almond syrup

1 ounce freshly squeezed lime juice

1 mint sprig, for garnish

1 lime wheel, for garnish

Pour all the liquid ingredients into a mixing glass. Add large cold ice cubes and shake vigorously for 7 or 8 seconds. Strain into a rocks glass over large cold ice cubes. Garnish with the mint sprig and lime wheel.

DOMINANT FLAVORS: aged rum and almond with fresh mint on the nose
BODY: medium with rich mouthfeel
DRYNESS: medium to off-dry
COMPLEXITY: medium

ACCENTUATING OR CONTRASTING FLAVORS: citrus, bitter orange peel
FINISH: medium, bittersweet with light oak and fruit overtones

GLASS: rocks

Tasting Notes

MATA HARI

The Mata Hari makes reference to the beautiful exotic dancer and alleged double agent of World War I who was wrongfully executed for spying and became the archetype for the term "femme fatale." In Malay, "mata hari" is the term for the sun, literally "eye of dawn." This sultry cocktail is a feast for all the senses; stunning to the eye, seductive on the nose, and orgasmic to the taste. We use Employees Only original Chai-Infused Sweet Vermouth with cognac, POM Wonderful pomegranate juice, and garnish with dried rose buds, which enhance its bouquet. The result is a cocktail as exotic and (supposedly) dangerous as its namesake. MAKES 1 DRINK

1¼ ounces Louis Royer Force 53 VSOP cognac

1 ounce Chai-Infused Sweet Vermouth (page 159)

¾ ounce freshly squeezed lemon juice

¾ ounce pomegranate juice

½ ounce simple syrup (page 154)

3 dried organic rose buds, for garnish

Pour the cognac, vermouth, juices, and syrup into a mixing glass. Add large cold ice cubes and shake vigorously. Strain into a chilled cocktail glass and garnish with rose buds.

Tasting Notes

DOMINANT FLAVORS: deep red pomegranates with roses on the nose
BODY: rich, full mouthfeel
DRYNESS: medium
COMPLEXITY: high

ACCENTUATING OR CONTRASTING FLAVORS: chai, cinnamon, and clove interweave
FINISH: lingering, black tea, spicy

GLASS: cocktail

CALVADOS SIDECAR

This is simply a playful variation on the classic Sidecar that we whip out from time to time for the right customer. Calvados is a French apple brandy treated with the same care as cognac. To play off the apple flavors, we added ground cinnamon to the sugar rim—a classic pairing with apples. MAKES 1 DRINK

Lemon wedge

4 tablespoons superfine sugar lightly speckled with ½ teaspoon fresh grated cinnamon, for rim

1 ounce Daron Fine calvados

1 ounce Cointreau

1 ounce freshly squeezed lemon juice

1 orange twist, for garnish

Moisten the rim of a cocktail glass with the lemon wedge. Carefully dip the rim in the cinnamon sugar so that only the very top edge is coated evenly. Place the glass in the freezer to let the sugar rim harden. Pour the calvados, Cointreau, and juice into a mixing glass. Add large cold ice cubes and shake vigorously. Strain into the prepared cocktail glass. Garnish with the orange twist.

DOMINANT FLAVORS: burned brandy and citrus with orange on the nose

BODY: rich, medium

DRYNESS: medium

COMPLEXITY: medium

ACCENTUATING OR CONTRASTING FLAVORS: cinnamon oak and sugar granules

FINISH: medium, slightly spicy with cinnamon bark and orange oil overtones

GLASS: cocktail

Tasting Notes

SIDECAR

The Sidecar is another famous cocktail that came out of Paris in the Twenties, thanks to Prohibition driving the best bartenders out of the country. It is said to have been invented at the Ritz Hotel by American ex-pat Frank Meyer, the head bartender. It was a favorite of Hemingway, F. Scott Fitzgerald, and Henry Miller. The Sidecar is also an ideal after-dinner option or even a nightcap because of its "candied" nature. Cognac is rarely mixed with juices, as the subtle qualities in fine brandy are easily lost in cocktails. The Sidecar is one exception—it blends cognac and Cointreau beautifully and balances them out with fresh lemon juice. The key to this cocktail is its sugar rim on the glass. This dissolves on the tongue and mixes with the rest of the drink to create the perfect balance, leaving room for the brandy. For a simple variation on the Sidecar, add a splash of Benedictine and lose the sugar rim to create the Honeymoon. MAKES 1 DRINK

Lemon wedge

Superfine sugar, for rim

1¼ ounces Courvoisier VS cognac

1¼ ounces Cointreau

1 ounce freshly squeezed lemon juice

1 orange twist, for garnish

Moisten the rim of a cocktail glass with the lemon wedge. Carefully dip the rim in the sugar so that only the very top edge is coated evenly. Place the glass in the freezer to let the sugar rim harden. Pour the cognac, Cointreau, and juice into a mixing glass. Add large cold ice cubes and shake vigorously. Strain into the prepared cocktail glass. Garnish with the orange twist.

DOMINANT FLAVORS: citrus, heavy on oranges with orange on the nose

BODY: medium, rich

DRYNESS: medium

COMPLEXITY: low to medium

ACCENTUATING OR CONTRASTING FLAVORS: sugar granules and oak

FINISH: short with orange oil and lemon overtones

GLASS: cocktail

Tasting Notes

MEDITERRA

This all-year-round cocktail, an Employees Only original, is a fine example of what you can do with a less-inspiring spirit like vodka. We wanted to combine traditional Mediterranean flavors such as figs, lemon, and honey. Mixing with vodka is a challenge similar to that of cooking with tofu; no matter what you do to it, it's still tofu. All the flavor and texture comes from the other ingredients in the mixture; vodka really contributes only alcohol to the structure of the cocktail. In the case of the Mediterra, any other spirit would interfere with the clean balance of fig to honey. MAKES 1 DRINK

2 ounces Luksusowa potato vodka

1 ounce Honey Syrup (page 155)

¾ ounce Boiron or homemade fig purée (see below)

½ ounce freshly squeezed lemon juice

Pour the vodka, syrup, purée, and juice into a mixing glass. Add large cold ice cubes and shake vigorously. Strain into a chilled cocktail glass.

FIG PURÉE

1 pound ripe Black Mission figs

1 tablespoon superfine sugar

1 ounce freshly squeezed lemon juice

2 ounces water

Combine all ingredients in a blender. Liquefy and strain through a coarse sieve. Refrigerate until use. Will keep for 4 days. MAKES ABOUT 1 CUP

Tasting Notes

DOMINANT FLAVORS: figs and honey
BODY: full, rich mouthfeel of fig meat
DRYNESS: medium to off-dry
COMPLEXITY: medium

ACCENTUATING OR CONTRASTING FLAVORS: citrus and vanilla
FINISH: medium, slightly bittersweet from fig seeds

GLASS: cocktail

BEE'S KNEES

Have you ever heard the slang term "the bee's knees"? It was used in the 1920s during the Noble Experiment to describe something really cool and hip. The cocktail itself appeared sometime during Prohibition. The recipe appears in cocktail books printed after 1936, which helps back this theory. It is fairly easy to make—the trick is to use honey syrup instead of honey itself, as honey will not dissolve when shaken with ice in a cocktail. We suggest Cadenhead's Old Raj saffron-infused gin, at 55 percent alcohol by volume. Some authorities claim this cocktail can also be made with rum. If you're game, we suggest the Flor de Caña four-year-old clear rum, which adds the perfect amount of grassiness and earthiness to the overall flavor profile. MAKES 1 DRINK

2 ounces Cadenhead's Old Raj gin 55

1 ounce Honey Syrup (page 155)

¾ ounce freshly squeezed lemon juice

1 lemon twist, for garnish

Pour the gin, syrup, and juice into a mixing glass. Add large cold ice cubes and shake vigorously. Strain into a chilled cocktail glass and garnish with the lemon twist.

DOMINANT FLAVORS: citrus and honey
BODY: mouthwateringly crisp
DRYNESS: medium
COMPLEXITY: medium

ACCENTUATING OR CONTRASTING FLAVORS: juniper and saffron
FINISH: medium with bitter orange overtones

GLASS: cocktail

Tasting Notes

PIMM'S CUP

Pimm's is a proprietary cocktail in a bottle created by James Pimm in 1820 for his London oyster bar. His first blend, Pimm's No. 1 Cup, was a gin-based liqueur infused with quinine, fruit extracts, and a secret blend of herbs. The word "cup" in this case refers to a punch made with spirits, wine, and soda or sparkling wine. Pimm started commercially offering Pimm's No. 1 Cup around 1859, and by the end of World War II five more bottled blends had been developed: Pimm's No. 2 Cup, based on Scotch whisky; No. 3, on brandy; No. 4, on rum; No. 5, on rye whiskey; and finally, No. 6, on vodka. Originally, most cups were garnished with cucumber or cucumber peel.

Employees Only pays tribute to this forgotten trend in our Pimm's Cup cocktail, which can be made as a long drink or in large batches or pitchers for parties. We build the base of the cocktail with Cointreau and fresh lime juice to add more alcohol and firm up the body. Fresh mint and delicious thinly sliced cucumbers are lightly bruised in the shake to release aroma, and we top it off with ginger ale, which adds to and opens up the bright flavors of the cocktail. MAKES 1 DRINK

2 ounces Pimm's No. 1 Cup	3 thin cucumber wheels
¾ ounce Cointreau	6 fresh mint leaves
¾ ounce freshly squeezed lime juice	1 ounce ginger ale

Pour the Pimm's, Cointreau, and lime juice into a Collins glass. Add the cucumbers and mint. Fill with large cold ice cubes and cover the glass with a small shaker top. Shake briefly and top off with ginger ale.

Tasting Notes

DOMINANT FLAVORS: Mint, basil, quinine, apples, and pears
BODY: refreshing, slightly sparkling
DRYNESS: medium
COMPLEXITY: medium with lots of subtle notes

ACCENTUATING OR CONTRASTING FLAVORS: cucumber, mint, and bright flavors pop out
FINISH: short, dry, citrus with lingering note of brandy

GLASS: Collins

CLASSIC PIMM'S CUP

Pimm's is as British as cricket or a cup of tea and has gained in recognition with the general rebirth of the classic cocktail. The original recipe for the Pimm's Cup is a very simple affair of Pimm's No. 1 and lemon-lime soda served over ice with slices of cucumber. The Brits refer to this simply as Pimm's and Lemonade ("lemonade" being the UK term for lemon-lime soda). What is fantastic about this recipe is the simplicity of ingredients. Add some cucumber and even a little mint and you have already elevated the cocktail. Try substituting champagne in the cocktail or even adding seasonal fruits to the mix, and you are light years beyond a simple highball.
MAKES 1 DRINK

2 ounces Pimm's No. 1 Cup

3 thin cucumber wheels

6 fresh mint leaves

3 ounces lemon-lime soda

Pour the Pimm's into a Collins glass. Add the cucumbers and mint and large cold ice cubes. Top off with the soda.

Tasting Notes

DOMINANT FLAVORS: candied oranges
BODY: very light, effervescent
DRYNESS: off-dry
COMPLEXITY: low

ACCENTUATING OR CONTRASTING FLAVORS: some herb; cucumber and mint shining
FINISH: short, fizzy

GLASS: Collins

GRINGO PISCO SOUR

We have served this variation of the Pisco Sour ever since we first learned about the drink in the mid-1990s. There weren't many Pisco choices available back then, so we worked with what we had. One brand we used was Pisco Capel Reservado from Chile, a blend of 30 percent Muscat and 70 percent Pedro Jimenez and Torontel grapes, which give the spirit a nice sweet full flavor, as it's aged in wood for up to 6 months. Because of the slight oak, it combines beautifully with fresh lemon juice, so our variation was a gringo-styled sour, tall over ice. Little did we know that the true Peruvian Pisco Sour (page 115) was created by a gringo as well. MAKES 1 DRINK

2 ounces Pisco Capel Reservado brandy

¾ ounce simple syrup (page 154)

¾ ounce freshly squeezed lemon juice

½ ounce freshly squeezed orange juice

1 egg white

3 dashes Angostura bitters, for garnish

1 orange half-wheel, for garnish

1 brandied cherry (see page 36), for garnish

Pour the brandy, syrup, juices, and egg white into a mixing glass. Close the shaker and shake very hard without ice for a few seconds. Add large cold ice cubes and shake vigorously for up to 30 seconds. Strain into a Collins glass filled with ice and garnish with the bitters, orange, and cherry.

DOMINANT FLAVORS: grape musk and citrus
BODY: creamy, chalky, chewy
DRYNESS: off-dry
COMPLEXITY: medium, subtle

ACCENTUATING OR CONTRASTING FLAVORS: Angostura bitters
FINISH: short, dry with citrus overtones

GLASS: Collins

Tasting Notes

PERUVIAN PISCO SOUR

The Pisco Sour is the official drink of Peru; there is even a National Pisco Sour Day, celebrated the first Saturday in February. Pisco brandy was first established by Spanish conquistadors, who planted grape vines as they traversed the mountainous terrains of Chile and Peru—and Chile also claims the Pisco as a national treasure. There is good reason for the debate, as Pisco was the first distilled spirit in the New World. The now-classic Pisco Sour was created in the 1920s by ex-pat American bartender Victor V. "Gringo" Morris at the Morris' Bar in Lima, as a local variation on the Whiskey Sour. The cocktail became a favorite among the locals and quickly spread up the West Coast of America as far north as San Francisco, where it was popular by the late 1930s. This version contained pisco brandy, egg white, lime juice, simple syrup, and aromatic bitters served frothy and straight up. A specific kind of lime called Limon de Pica is the right ingredient for the Peruvian classic. Some places in Peru grate nutmeg or cinnamon on top of the cocktail to finish it; our version includes the nutmeg. The Peruvian Pisco Sour is the perfect brunch companion as a restorative drink: musky and clean, with a rich texture and alluring bitters.   MAKES 1 DRINK

2 ounces Barsol Pisco Quebranta brandy

¾ ounce freshly squeezed lime juice

¾ ounce simple syrup (page 154)

1 egg white

3 drops Angostura bitters, for garnish

Freshly grated nutmeg, for garnish

Pour the brandy, juice, syrup, and egg white into a mixing glass. Close the shaker and shake very hard without ice for a few seconds. Add large cold ice cubes and shake vigorously for up to 30 seconds. Strain into a chilled cocktail glass and garnish with the bitters and freshly grated nutmeg.

DOMINANT FLAVORS: grape musk and lime
BODY: creamy, rich mouthfeel
DRYNESS: medium
COMPLEXITY: high, very subtle

ACCENTUATING OR CONTRASTING FLAVORS: nutmeg and aromatics
FINISH: short, soft, dry

GLASS: cocktail

Tasting Notes

PISCO PUNCH

Pisco became popular on the West Coast, especially in San Francisco, during the days of the Gold Rush. Many ships would bring men from the East Coast around Cape Horn, through the Strait of Magellan and up the West Coast. One of the stops for provisions was the popular port town of Pisco. There they would load up on the eponymous brandy and bring whatever was left with them to Northern California. Soon the spirit became a commodity on the trade route of the western seaboard. (This would, of course, later decline with the creation of the Panama Canal cutting Peru out of the route.) The Pisco Punch was created during the late 1800s by a barkeep named Duncan Nicol at the Bank Exchange and Billiard Saloon in San Francisco. The exact recipe was never shared with anyone but was enjoyed by the likes of Mark Twain and Jack London. After Nicol's passing, those who knew offered up their interpretations of the Pisco Punch. MAKES 1 DRINK

2 1-inch cubes fresh pineapple

1½ ounces Fresh Pineapple Syrup (page 156)

2 ounces Barsol Pisco Quebranta brandy

½ ounce freshly squeezed lemon juice

½ ounce freshly squeezed lime juice

5 drops Bitter Truth Celery Bitters

1 lemon wheel

1 pineapple wedge, skin on, for garnish

Muddle the pineapple cubes and pineapple syrup in the bottom of a mixing glass. Add the brandy, juices, bitters, and large cold ice cubes. Shake vigorously for 7 or 8 seconds and strain into a large wine goblet over large cold ice cubes. Drop in the lemon wheel and garnish the rim with the pineapple wedge.

Tasting Notes

DOMINANT FLAVORS: pineapple and grape musk

BODY: medium, fibrous, full mouthfeel

DRYNESS: medium to dry

COMPLEXITY: medium

ACCENTUATING OR CONTRASTING FLAVORS: celery and grass

FINISH: short, dry, mouthwatering

GLASS: large wine goblet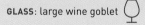

QUIET STORM

Inspiration for the Quiet Storm comes from hot, steamy New York City summer days. EO bartender Milos Zica wanted to find a refreshing bourbon cocktail that would transcend age and gender. His journey began by creating an infusion using T Salon's Silence tea, made from rooibos or South African red bush tea with roses, vanilla, orange, and almonds—ingredients all known for their soothing properties. He steeped it in bianco or sweet white vermouth to help retain the softer flavors while showcasing the terra-cotta hue of the tea. Finished with ginger beer, lemon juice, and simple syrup, this drink lives up to its intended purpose as an elegant yet simple refreshing whiskey cocktail. The name hints at the Silence tea moniker while also hinting at the ginger beer found in a Dark and Stormy (page 120). MAKES 1 DRINK

1½ ounces Maker's Mark bourbon

1 ounce Red Bush–Infused Vermouth (page 159)

¾ ounce freshly squeezed lemon juice

½ ounce simple syrup (page 154)

3 ounces Spicy Ginger Beer (page 156) or Fever-Tree ginger beer

1 lemon wheel, for garnish

1 mint sprig, for garnish

Build the drink by pouring the bourbon, vermouth, juice, and syrup into a tall Collins glass. Fill up with large cold ice cubes and cover the glass with a small shaker top. Shake briefly, remove the shaker top, and top off with ginger beer. Garnish with the lemon wheel and mint sprig.

DARK AND STORMY

Dark and Stormy was created specifically for Gosling's Black Seal rum in much the same way that the Moscow Mule was created for Smirnoff. The original recipe called for Gosling's, ginger beer, and a lime. This simple com-bination works very well to create an interesting highball, but to expand on its potential, many mixologists have reconstructed it, and its popularity has approached that of the mojito. Over the years, we have created many recipes for our Dark and Stormy, using varying ingredients such as fresh gingerroot, lime juice, and even walnut liqueur. Today, we have settled on using dark rum, homemade ginger beer, and lime juice with the addition of Velvet Falernum—a clove-almond–flavored liqueur that bridges the flavors of molasses and fiery ginger. MAKES 1 DRINK

½ ounce John D. Taylor's Velvet Falernum liqueur

½ ounce freshly squeezed lime juice

1 lime wheel

4 ounces Spicy Ginger Beer (page 156) or Fever-Tree ginger beer

2 ounces Gosling's Black Seal rum

Pour the liqueur and juice into a Collins glass. Add large cold ice cubes and the lime wheel. Cover the glass with a small shaker and shake briefly. Fill with the ginger beer to one inch below the rim. Slowly layer the rum on top.

Tasting Notes

DOMINANT FLAVORS: ginger and molasses
BODY: light, refreshing
DRYNESS: medium with ginger dryness
COMPLEXITY: robust

ACCENTUATING OR CONTRASTING FLAVORS: clove and bitterness from lime
FINISH: medium with ginger overtones

GLASS: Collins

The Moscow Mule became the flagship drink for Smirnoff vodka in the 1950s and started the vodka craze in the United States. Previously, vodka was not widely known. But this cocktail saved a vodka distillery and a restaurant in West Hollywood from going bankrupt. The first American vodka distillery was started in Connecticut by John G. Martin, using a recipe he acquired in Paris from Pierre Smirnoff. For fifteen years, vodka sales were minuscule, and the Smirnoff vodka was known as "Martin's Folly." At the Cock 'n' Bull restaurant on Hollywood's Sunset Strip, Martin met the owner, Jack Morgan, who was sitting on a large quantity of ginger beer he had produced under his restaurant's name. Coincidentally, Morgan was also about to lose his shirt. With both sitting on a large stock of unsold product, the myth is that they got drunk and decided to marry their miseries with a squeeze of lime. They named the concoction Moscow Mule because of the kick of the ginger. They served the new drink in a personally engraved copper mug to every movie star, and it became an overnight smash. Cold War controversy added to the appeal among the liberal Hollywood bons vivants. But it wasn't long before vodka outshone the cocktail that had given it celebrity. Once Zsa Zsa Gabor declared that she only drank Martinis made with Smirnoff, vodka sales soared. MAKES 1 DRINK

2 ounces Smirnoff vodka

½ ounce freshly squeezed lime juice

4½ ounces Spicy Ginger Beer (page 156) or Fever-Tree ginger beer

1 lime wheel, for garnish

Pour the vodka and juice into a Collins glass filled with large cold ice cubes. Fill with ginger beer. Stir gently. Drop in the lime wheel.

DOMINANT FLAVORS: ginger
BODY: crisp, light
DRYNESS: dry to medium
COMPLEXITY: low, straightforward ginger flavor

ACCENTUATING OR CONTRASTING FLAVORS: lime juice brings balance
FINISH: short with spicy overtones

GLASS: Collins

Tasting Notes

RUBY TUESDAY

This cocktail was first made on a Tuesday with the namesake song from the Rolling Stones playing in the background. When the drink was strained into a cocktail glass and its vibrant ruby beauty came to life, we said in unison, "Ruby Tuesday." This cocktail combines 101-proof straight rye whiskey, Benedictine, fresh black cherry purée, fresh lemon juice, and simple syrup. Rye whiskey is the native spirit of the northern United States, where rye grains grow in abundance. The spirit was traditionally matured in new American oak barrels and bottled at least 50 percent alcohol by volume (ABV) or 100-proof. Its raw nature, combined with slightly sweet overtones and the herbal infusion of Benedictine, give this cocktail a beautiful long, lingering finish. It is a perfect representative of such classy whiskey cocktails as the Frisco Sour. MAKES 1 DRINK

1½ ounces Wild Turkey 101-proof rye whiskey

1 ounce Benedictine

¾ ounce freshly squeezed lemon juice

½ ounce simple syrup (page 154)

¾ ounce Boiron black cherry purée or 5 ripe black cherries, muddled

1 lemon twist, for garnish

Pour the whiskey, Benedictine, juice, syrup, and purée into a mixing glass. Add large cold ice cubes and shake vigorously. Strain into a chilled cocktail glass and garnish with the lemon twist.

Tasting Notes

DOMINANT FLAVORS: ripe black cherries with a whiskey nose
BODY: full, rich mouthfeel
DRYNESS: medium
COMPLEXITY: medium to high

ACCENTUATING OR CONTRASTING FLAVORS: bold contrasts among fruit, whiskey, and Benedictine's honey and herbs
FINISH: long, honeyed with tannic cherry skin overtones

GLASS: cocktail

We were surprised to discover the Frisco Sour, as it was so close in ingredients to our Ruby Tuesday cocktail. This very tasty cocktail provides a multidimensional gastronomical experience. We serve it mainly to people who are exploring whiskey cocktails other than Manhattans and traditional sours. We have little information about this savory cocktail besides its recipe as it appears in Charles Schumann's American Bar *and later editions of* Mr. Boston. MAKES 1 DRINK

2 ounces Sazerac rye whiskey

1 ounce Benedictine

¾ ounce freshly squeezed lemon juice

½ ounce freshly squeezed lime juice

1 splash simple syrup (page 154)

1 lemon wheel, for garnish

1 lime wheel, for garnish

1 brandied cherry (see page 36), for garnish

Pour the whiskey, Benedictine, juices, and syrup into a mixing glass. Add large cold ice cubes and shake vigorously. Strain into a chilled cocktail glass and garnish with the lemon, lime, and cherry.

DOMINANT FLAVORS: whiskey and citrus on the nose
BODY: medium rich mouthfeel
DRYNESS: medium, perfectly balanced
COMPLEXITY: medium

ACCENTUATING OR CONTRASTING FLAVORS: honey, oak, and herbs poke out of the citrus blast
FINISH: short, fruity citrus

GLASS: cocktail

Tasting Notes

STEVE-O'S TUXEDO

This is a cocktail that was composed by one of our bartenders, former U.S. Marine Steve Schneider. According to him, he got tired of mixing White Ladies and wanted something more exciting and powerful to offer as a gin cocktail. When asked to describe his intention, he simply said: "Alongside a beautiful lady should be a handsome man in a tux. By replacing Cointreau with a touch of simple syrup and orange bitters, you are getting an easy, yet stunning White Lady variation, which is more appealing to the modern palate." MAKES 1 DRINK

1¾ ounces Plymouth gin

1 egg white

¾ ounce freshly squeezed lemon juice

½ ounce simple syrup (page 154)

1 dash Regan's Orange Bitters No.6

1 orange twist, for garnish

Pour the gin, egg white, juice, syrup, and bitters into a mixing glass. Add large cold ice cubes and shake vigorously for at least 45 seconds. Strain into a chilled cocktail glass and garnish with the orange twist.

Tasting Notes

DOMINANT FLAVORS: juniper
BODY: creamy, medium
DRYNESS: medium to dry
COMPLEXITY: low to medium

ACCENTUATING OR CONTRASTING FLAVORS: roasted orange oils
FINISH: medium, crisp

GLASS: cocktail

WHITE LADY

This Prohibition-era cocktail is not very ladylike on the surface. On paper, it looks like a Sidecar made with gin, but nothing could be farther from the truth. We tasted this cocktail at the Savoy in London where it was invented, according to Harry Craddock, author of The Savoy Cocktail Book, *which was published in 1930. Three high-quality ingredients and a master technique make this cocktail a high point of everyone's evening. We suggest you pack your freezer full of large ice cubes, squeeze a lot of fresh lemon juice, and get going. Play some slapstick movies while you drink it—it is said that this cocktail was the favorite of Laurel and Hardy.*
MAKES 1 DRINK

1¾ ounces Plymouth gin

1¼ ounces Cointreau

1 ounce freshly squeezed lemon juice

1 orange twist, for garnish

Pour the gin, Cointreau, and juice into a mixing glass. Add large cold ice cubes and shake vigorously. Strain into a chilled cocktail glass and garnish with the orange twist.

Ah, Waterloo—the monarch of Employees Only long drinks. Seasonal to the core and perfect from mid-June until early September when watermelons are in their prime. This cocktail combines fresh, ripe watermelon; gin; and Campari in a taste explosion. The most important ingredient is the watermelon, as the flavor directly corresponds to the sweetness of the cocktail. Therefore we advise you to use organic watermelon with seeds rather than the genetically engineered seedless varietals. The seeds also provide a nice visual touch when the cocktail is served. This cocktail is also a great exercise in mixing and building flavors. You start with fresh fruit, add sugar to open up the natural flavors, then add sour to balance it out. Altogether, this mixture creates a pumped-up watermelon bomb with the body to stand up to even gin. The gin and Campari bring out the savoriness of the melon to make this cocktail a modern classic.   MAKES 1 DRINK

4 (1 x 2-inch) chunks of watermelon

¾ ounce simple syrup (page 154)

1½ ounces Plymouth gin

½ ounce freshly squeezed lemon juice

½ ounce Campari

1 watermelon wedge, with rind, for garnish

Muddle the watermelon chunks and syrup in the bottom of a mixing glass until the fruit has turned into a juice. Then add the gin, juice, and Campari and fill the glass with 5 large cold ice cubes. Shake briefly and pour unstrained into a tall Collins glass. Garnish with the watermelon wedge.

DOMINANT FLAVORS: watermelon and fragrant juniper
BODY: medium to light
DRYNESS: medium
COMPLEXITY: medium

ACCENTUATING OR CONTRASTING FLAVORS: high contrast between soft watermelon and bitter Campari
FINISH: medium, bittersweet

GLASS: Collins

Tasting Notes

WEST SIDE

f
o

This cocktail is an Employees Only variation of the famous South Side cocktail (page 130), first served in the 1920s at the New York speakeasy Jack & Charlie's—now known as the 21 Club. We replaced the gin with Meyer lemon–infused vodka to achieve a more balanced, subtler concoction. God only knows how many West Sides we have pushed over the bar in the last five years. It is by far the most popular cocktail served at Employees Only and lends itself naturally to being enjoyed in the sun. Why is this cocktail so popular? Even if we ignore the fact that it is a vodka cocktail and the fact that we are witnessing the end of the reign of vodka, the simplicity of a cocktail with just lemon and mint flavors makes it addictive and refreshing. It will definitely be a favorite at any cocktail party, served over ice or in pitchers. MAKES 1 DRINK

2 ounces Charbay Meyer lemon vodka

1 ounce freshly squeezed lemon juice

½ ounce simple syrup (page 154)

3-finger pinch fresh mint leaves

1 splash club soda

Put the vodka, juice, syrup, and mint in a mixing glass. Add large cold ice cubes and shake vigorously. Open the shaker and add the club soda. Use a julep strainer to strain into a chilled cocktail glass.

SOUTH SIDE

Also known as South Side Fizz, the South Side seems to have first been published by famous American bartender Harry Craddock in The Savoy Cocktail Book. *His recipe called for dry gin, powdered sugar, the juice of half a lemon, and two sprigs of fresh mint, finished with a splash of siphon soda water. The birthplace is disputed among Jack & Charlie's (now the 21 Club) in New York City, a forgotten speakeasy in the South Side of Chicago, and a Long Island country club in the late 1800s known as the Southside Club. There is no controversy that the 21 Club has served more of these than anyone over the decades and they can lay claim to the South Side as their house cocktail. We've altered it a bit by replacing the powdered sugar with simple syrup and adding a splash of soda to the cocktail to "wake it up," as some recipes dictate. We do not recommend double straining it; that would reduce the body and the ornamental presence of the shaken mint.*   MAKES 1 DRINK

2 ounces Plymouth gin

1 ounce freshly squeezed lemon juice

½ ounce simple syrup (page 154)

2 mint sprigs

1 splash club soda

Put the gin, juice, syrup, and mint in a mixing glass. Add large cold ice cubes and shake vigorously. Open the shaker and add the club soda. Use a julep strainer to strain into a chilled cocktail glass.

Tasting Notes

DOMINANT FLAVORS: juniper-citrus bomb
BODY: crisp, slightly effervescent
DRYNESS: medium to dry
COMPLEXITY: low

ACCENTUATING OR CONTRASTING FLAVORS: mint and Meyer lemon rind make this cocktail sing
FINISH: short, clean, crisp

GLASS: cocktail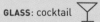

YELLOW JACKET

The Yellow Jacket cocktail was inspired by chance circumstances and a little harassment. For weeks, we had toyed with the idea of mixing together Partida Reposado tequila and St-Germain elderflower liqueur, but there was a piece of the puzzle missing. Then one evening, a bunch of obnoxious cocktail geeks came into Employees Only to stump the bartenders by ordering the Last Word cocktail. After being satisfied with that drink, they asked if we knew of another drink with Chartreuse. At that moment, Yellow Chartreuse became the ingredient needed to bind together the elderflower and tequila. So pretty and elegant, the rich yellow color grabs your attention. The true beauty of this drink, though, is the interplay of the ingredients. The light oak on the Partida Reposado tequila works so well with the St-Germain, and they in turn produce a perfect ground for Yellow Chartreuse to bring it all into balance. The orange bitters play a key role. This cocktail is similar in style to the Widow's Kiss cocktail (page 141), as they both contain very sweet herbaceous ingredients balanced by high alcohol content. It's named for the yellow jacket wasps that inhabit agave farms and tequila distilleries. MAKES 1 DRINK

2 ounces Partida Reposado tequila

1 ounce St-Germain elderflower liqueur

¾ ounce Yellow Chartreuse

1 dash Regan's Orange Bitters No. 6

1 lemon twist, for garnish

Pour the tequila, liqueur, Chartreuse, and bitters into a mixing glass. Add large cold ice cubes and stir for 40 revolutions. Strain into a chilled cocktail glass. Garnish with the lemon twist.

DOMINANT FLAVORS: lemon oil on the nose followed by roasted agave
BODY: full, honeyed mouthfeel
DRYNESS: medium to off-dry
COMPLEXITY: high

ACCENTUATING OR CONTRASTING FLAVORS: floral, earthy, and herbal notes surround agave
FINISH: long, honeyed with slight bitter orange overtones

GLASS: cocktail

Tasting Notes

BELLINI

The story of the Bellini begins during Prohibition with American playboy Harry Pickering, who drank at the Europa Hotel in Venice with bartender Giuseppe Cipriani. Pickering's family had cut off his funds in a last-ditch effort to get him back home and quit drinking. Pickering asked Cipriani for a loan of 10,000 lire—the equivalent of $61,000 today—to get his affairs in order. Cipriani lent him his life savings, only to not hear a word from Pickering for over a year. Legend has it that when Pickering returned to the bar, he ordered a drink and paid Cipriani 50,000 lire as a show of gratitude so he could open his own bar. In 1931, Harry's Bar in Venice opened and the Bellini cocktail was created there shortly afterward. MAKES 1 DRINK

1 ounce Boiron or homemade white peach purée (see below)

4½ ounces chilled Zardetto Prosecco

½ ounce Massenez crème de pêche or peach liqueur

Pour the peach purée into a mixing glass. While stirring, slowly add the Prosecco. Drizzle in the peach liqueur to reduce the foam. Pour into a chilled champagne flute.

WHITE PEACH PURÉE

4 fresh white peaches, skin on, cut in half and pitted

8 raspberries

4 tablespoons superfine sugar

2 ounces water

2 ounces freshly squeezed lemon juice

Combine all ingredients in a blender. Liquefy to consistency. Keep refrigerated until use. Will keep for 3 days. MAKES ABOUT 2 CUPS

Tasting Notes

DOMINANT FLAVORS: white peaches
BODY: medium, velvety, vibrant texture
DRYNESS: medium
COMPLEXITY: low, fruit forward

ACCENTUATING OR CONTRASTING FLAVORS: peach cordial balances the acidity of the Prosecco
FINISH: short, sweet and fruity

GLASS: champagne flute

BLOOD PEACH BELLINI

Blood peaches are large, with dark red skin surrounding a rich, crimson, juicy flesh that is quite tart. They bruise easily, so they are frequently broken down for use in chutneys, jams, pastries, ice creams, and sorbets. We figured this would also mean that they were ideal for making cocktails. The Bellini was the obvious choice as our first guinea pig. We accentuated the bitterness of the fruit with a little Campari while also increasing the intensity of the color. The result is a refreshing eye-opener with slight bitterness and charm. Blood peaches are very rare, fresh or frozen, so if you can get your hands on them, grab them. You can also make this cocktail by blending white peach purée with EO homemade Grenadine for color. MAKES 1 DRINK

1 ounce Boiron or homemade White Peach Purée (opposite page)

¼ ounce homemade Grenadine (page 157)

4½ ounces chilled Prosecco

¼ ounce Campari

Pour the peach purée and grenadine into a mixing glass. While stirring, slowly add the Prosecco. Drizzle in the Campari to reduce the foam. Pour into a chilled champagne flute.

DOMINANT FLAVORS: tart peach fruit forward
BODY: medium, velvety, vibrant texture
DRYNESS: medium acidity from Prosecco
COMPLEXITY: medium

ACCENTUATING OR CONTRASTING FLAVORS: Campari adds depth and bitterness
FINISH: long, bittersweet

GLASS: champagne flute

Tasting Notes

BLOODY MARY

The Bloody Mary is by far the most universally known pick-me-up. Legend has it that the Bloody Mary was born in Paris in or around 1921 at Harry's New York Bar by a Frenchman, Fernand "Pete" Petiot. In those days, it consisted merely of a shot of vodka mixed with tomato juice and maybe a squeeze of lemon. MAKES 1 DRINK

2 ounces Russian Standard vodka

5 ounces Bloody Mary mix (recipe follows)

½ ounce freshly squeezed lemon juice

1 long celery stalk, for garnish

1 lemon wedge, for garnish

Grape tomato, pickled onion, olive on a skewer, for garnish

Pour the vodka, mix, and juice into a Collins glass. Add large cold ice cubes and shake briefly to blend. Garnish with the celery, lemon, and tomato-onion-olive skewer.

BLOODY MARY MIX

3 cups tomato juice

½ tablespoon capers, crushed

3 ounces Worcestershire sauce

2 ounces freshly squeezed lemon juice

1 ounce olive brine

½ teaspoon celery salt

1 teaspoon freshly ground black pepper

1 teaspoon Tabasco

4 tablespoons freshly grated horseradish

Stir all ingredients in a large food-safe container until well combined. Refrigerate overnight. Stir again before using. Will keep for 3 days, refrigerated. MAKES 1 QUART

Tasting Notes

DOMINANT FLAVORS: tomato, pepper sauce, and lemon
BODY: full-textured
DRYNESS: medium to dry
COMPLEXITY: high

ACCENTUATING OR CONTRASTING FLAVORS: capers, horseradish, and black pepper
FINISH: short, salty with lingering spiciness

GLASS: rocks

MID-MORNING FIZZ

The Mid-Morning Fizz is our take on the classic Ramos Gin Fizz and is our choice for the perfect summer eye-opener. Our variation loses the cream of the original recipe and adds Green Chartreuse for a more pronounced spiciness. It is a lighter but more complex cocktail and loves to pair with traditional brunch grub like croque monsieur, burgers, steak and eggs, and especially French toast. Like all cocktails containing egg whites, the Mid-Morning Fizz requires a long, hard, and steady shake. MAKES 1 DRINK

½ ounce Green Chartreuse

1 ounce club soda

1¾ ounces Martin Miller's Westbourne Strength 100-proof gin

1 ounce freshly squeezed lemon juice

¾ ounce simple syrup (page 154)

5 drops orange blossom water

1 egg white

1 orange half-wheel, for garnish

Pour the Chartreuse into the bottom of a Collins glass. Fill with large cold ice cubes and add the club soda. Place the glass in the freezer. Combine the gin, juice, syrup, orange blossom water, and egg white in a mixing glass. Add large cold ice cubes and shake vigorously for at least 2 minutes to make sure the cocktail has sufficient texture and frothiness. To achieve a layered effect, strain carefully over the chilled Chartreuse. Garnish with the orange.

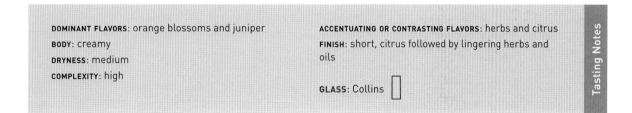

DOMINANT FLAVORS: orange blossoms and juniper
BODY: creamy
DRYNESS: medium
COMPLEXITY: high

ACCENTUATING OR CONTRASTING FLAVORS: herbs and citrus
FINISH: short, citrus followed by lingering herbs and oils

GLASS: Collins

Tasting Notes

RAMOS GIN FIZZ

This frothy and very yummy long drink was invented in 1888 by Henry C. Ramos, bartender at Meyer's Restaurant in New Orleans. Because the cocktail requires a lot of shaking, the bar used to hire so-called "shaker boys," who would just shake one cocktail after another in times of heavy business. The Ramos Gin Fizz is a full-blown classic nowadays and is ordered regularly all the time, but it was intended to be enjoyed as a pick-me-up or an eye-opener. Meaning—in the morning. Shocking, isn't it, how our forefathers used to drink? The key ingredient is the orange blossom water; just those few drops give the cocktail its definitive character. Widely popularized before, during, and after Prohibition at the Roosevelt Hotel in New Orleans, it has spawned countless variations—and it's still enjoyed on porches across the South as the sun is setting. MAKES 1 DRINK

1 ounce club soda

1¾ ounces Martin Miller's Westbourne Strength 100-proof gin

1 ounce freshly squeezed lemon juice

¾ ounce simple syrup (page 154)

5 drops orange blossom water

1 egg white

¾ ounce heavy cream

Fill a Collins glass with large cold ice cubes and add the club soda. Place the glass in the freezer. Combine the gin, juice, syrup, orange blossom water, egg white, and cream in a mixing glass. Add large cold ice cubes and shake vigorously for at least 2 minutes to make sure that the cocktail has sufficient texture and frothiness. Strain carefully into the prepared Collins glass.

Tasting Notes

DOMINANT FLAVORS: orange blossom and juniper
BODY: creamy, rich mouthfeel
DRYNESS: medium to off-dry
COMPLEXITY: medium to high

ACCENTUATING OR CONTRASTING FLAVORS: floral notes and citrus mixed with sweet cream
FINISH: short, citrus followed by fragrant orange oils

GLASS: Collins

WIDOW'S KISS

According to cocktail historians, this cocktail first appeared in print in 1895 in Modern American Drinks *by George J. Kappeler. Although this drink has fallen into obscurity today, it appeared in every respectable cocktail book printed in the early twentieth century, with the same easy recipe. It seems this drink always had the favor of knowledgeable bartenders and connoisseurs, as its unique blend of flavors could be very challenging to the untrained palate of the casual drinker. In other words, this drink is best recommended for people who have moved beyond simple straightforward flavors and are looking for a carnival in the mouth. The Widow's Kiss is a seasonal experience best enjoyed when it is cold outside. This classic cocktail is also one of the few cocktails we recommend as a digestive or an after-dinner cocktail.* MAKES 1 DRINK

1½ ounces Daron Fine calvados

1¼ ounces Yellow Chartreuse

1¼ ounces Benedictine

1 dash Angostura bitters

1 lemon twist, for garnish

Pour the calvados, Chartreuse, Benedictine, and bitters into a mixing glass. Add large cold ice cubes and stir for 40 revolutions. Strain into a chilled cocktail glass. Garnish with the lemon twist.

DOMINANT FLAVORS: sweet herbal bouquet
BODY: high alcohol with heavy syrupy mouthfeel
DRYNESS: off-dry to sweet
COMPLEXITY: high, forceful

ACCENTUATING OR CONTRASTING FLAVORS: big herb bomb
FINISH: long, honey with citrus oil overtones
GLASS: cocktail

Tasting Notes

THE LAST WORD

Who will have the last word? Well, obviously, the bartender! We always have the last word, because we have the goodies—the booze. So when an experienced bartender says something to you, listen, because it may well be a recommendation for this tasty cocktail. The Last Word is a mishmash of high-octane fuels, yet it comes out surprisingly balanced and delicate. Beware: have too many and this cocktail will have the last word. Allegedly this Prohibition-era cocktail's origins are traced back to the Detroit Athletic Club, where it was invented by a gentleman named Frank Fogarty. He was said to be "a very fine monologue artist," which is probably how the drink got its name. One thing is certain: this cocktail is now in the top five of cocktail geekdom, appearing in bars all over the country. Made properly, it is truly a wonderful concoction. MAKES 1 DRINK

1 ounce Beefeater 24 gin

1 ounce Green Chartreuse

1 ounce Luxardo maraschino liqueur

1 ounce freshly squeezed lime juice

1 lime wheel, for garnish

Pour the gin, Chartreuse, liqueur, and juice into a mixing glass. Add large cold ice cubes and shake vigorously. Strain into a chilled cocktail glass and garnish with the lime wheel.

DOMINANT FLAVORS: lime and sour cherry
BODY: medium to full, invigorating mouthfeel
DRYNESS: off-dry
COMPLEXITY: high

ACCENTUATING OR CONTRASTING FLAVORS: fruits against herbs and juniper
FINISH: lingering, dry with citrus overtones

GLASS: cocktail

Tasting Notes

PITCHERS, PUNCHES, AND SANGRIAS

I N A BUSY PLACE LIKE EMPLOYEES ONLY, there are few opportunities to serve punches or sangrias during regular dinner service. However, there are special events, like our annual End of Prohibition party, that provide the perfect occasion to showcase our punch-making and -serving skills. We like to give our punches a touch of our magic, to deepen the flavor or bring everything into balance. Although on paper these drinks calling for many bottles of distilled spirits and wine may look scary, they are in fact really easy to make. In most cases, you make your punch at least a few hours before serving time, so you can play with the recipe to your liking and the flavors can meld. Our recipes are guidelines. We suggest you first follow the recipe, then taste. If you are happy, great; if not start adding whatever you might think could improve the taste; please tailor them to your own taste. Do not forget that punches must start with a slightly higher alcoholic content than cocktails; they will dilute over time as the ice blocks melt. Keep in mind, though, it is always easier to add more alcohol than to take it out. With that, we wish you a beautiful punch-making experience. Cheers!

PIMM'S FRUIT CUP

This is a party version of the Pimm's Cup (pages 114 and 116), for when you want to give your guests a break during a three-day cricket match marathon. The difference is you have a few more fresh fruits at your disposal. We find it tastes best if in addition to the cucumber and mint you add strawberries, diced apples, and orange half-wheels. Then again, you can experiment for yourself and play with some seasonal fruits. Maybe some pears will give it your special touch; gin and pears mix really well. When preparing the large-batch cocktail, try to press the fruits and herbs very gently. It's essential that you mix the large batch several hours ahead—ideally, the night before your guests arrive. Refrigerate it to let the fruits steep and release their essence into the blend.
MAKES 2 QUARTS

35 fresh mint leaves

2 cups Pimm's No. 1 Cup

¾ cup Cointreau

¾ cup freshly squeezed lime juice

20 thin cucumber wheels

10 strawberries cut into quarters

½ apple cut into thin slices (optional)

½ Bartlett pear, cut into thin slices (optional)

2 cups ginger ale

Put the mint leaves into a large pitcher or smaller punch bowl and gently tap them with a muddler or small ladle to extract the essence. Add the Pimm's, Cointreau, juice, cucumbers, strawberries, apple, and pear and stir to combine. Cover with a lid or plastic wrap and refrigerate overnight. Just before serving, add large cold ice cubes and the ginger ale. Gently stir and serve in individual cups.

WEST SIDE PUNCH

This punch is simple, easy, and highly refreshing. It was born out of necessity when we opened for brunch and had to serve tons of our West Side cocktails to the girls brunching in our garden. The solution was simple and a win-win for us and the guests. We love to recommend this punch in the summertime; its flavors and crispness will freshen up the nastiest hangover. Perfect for weddings, bar mitzvahs, bridal and baby showers, and all those cute get-togethers people have. MAKES 1½ QUARTS

30 fresh mint leaves, no stems

1¾ cups Charbay Meyer lemon vodka

1 cup freshly squeezed lemon juice

⅔ cup simple syrup (page 154)

1 cup club soda

In the bottom of a large pitcher, bruise the mint leaves slightly with a ladle or muddler. Add the vodka, juice, and syrup. Stir gently and add the club soda. Fill the pitcher with ice and stir again for 1 minute. Serve immediately.

DECORATIVE ICE BLOCK FOR PUNCH

An easy way to dress up your punch is to make a decorative ice block. A Bundt cake pan (or any other interesting shape pan) can be used as a mold to make a large block of ice that is also functional. Be sure that whatever size mold you choose will fit into both your freezer and your punch bowl. Take thinly sliced citrus wheels or any of the other fruits in the punch recipe and scatter them evenly on the bottom of the pan. Fill the pan tightly with ice cubes to hold the fruit in place. Fill with cold water and place in the freezer for a few hours. Remove from the freezer just before serving. Hold the pan upside down under a stream of hot water briefly to separate the ice from the mold. The resulting ice should have fruits ornamenting the block. Look out, Martha!

JERSEY CITY FISH HOUSE PUNCH

This is one of our End of Prohibition party special punch recipes and it was adapted from the Philadelphia Fish House punch, which was a favorite of Generals Washington and Lafayette. We replaced the original cognac with our local Laird's AppleJack and got something fantastic as a result. We use all seasonal fruits for this—a beautiful feature that also makes it extra tasty. MAKES 5¾ QUARTS

Decorative ice block (opposite page)

6 Fuji apples, diced

6 large Bartlett pears, diced

6 lemons, cut into half-wheels

6 limes, cut into half-wheels

3 cups Smith & Cross Traditional Jamaica rum

1 quart Laird's AppleJack

1 quart freshly squeezed lemon juice

2 quarts water

¾ cup Massenez crème de pêche or peach liqueur

Prepare the decorative ice block, allowing a few hours for freezing.

Combine the fruits in a large punch bowl and add the rum, AppleJack, juice, water, and liqueur. Refrigerate for at least 4 to 5 hours. Just before serving, add the decorative ice block.

GIN PUNCH

We found this recipe in Jerry Thomas's 1862 How to Mix Drinks or the Bon Vivant's Companion, *in a recipe for a single serving. It called for Holland gin—or genever, as we know it today—and was probably a very popular drink.*

The back story is that when planning our first End of Prohibition party we were searching for punch recipes that could be served in teacups. So we started going through books and shot a few ideas back and forth until we found papa Jerry's recipe. We replaced the genever with Plymouth gin, and with a few more tweaks we got it perfect. The decorative ice block adds a great visual effect. MAKES 5 ¾ QUARTS

Decorative ice block (page 146)

6 navel oranges, cut into quarter-wheels

6 lemons, cut into half-wheels

3 limes, cut into wheels

1 pint fresh raspberries

1 pineapple, cut into 1-inch cubes

1 (750 ml) bottle Plymouth gin

1¾ cups freshly squeezed lemon juice

1¼ cups simple syrup (page 154)

½ cup orgeat or almond syrup

1 cup Massenez crème de framboise

3 cups water

1 (750 ml) bottle Perrier-Jouët Grand Brut champagne

Prepare the decorative ice block, allowing a few hours for freezing.

Combine all the fruits in a large punch bowl. Add the gin, juice, syrups, crème de framboise, and water. Refrigerate for at least 4 to 5 hours. Just before serving, add the champagne and the decorative ice block.

SPICED SANGRIA ROJA

This is our favorite sangria recipe—it involves a little more effort than the usual sangria, but its flavor is far more complex than just wine mixed with orange juice. It really should be enjoyed with food, preferably tapas and small plates. It is an excellent companion to cheese and fish as well.   MAKES 2 QUARTS

2 cups water

1 cup sugar

2 whole cloves

2 cinnamon sticks

2 star anise

1 vanilla pod, split

3 thin slices fresh ginger

1 (750 ml) bottle Rioja or dry Spanish red wine

1 cup freshly squeezed orange juice

⅛ cup freshly squeezed lime juice

1 orange, cut into quarter-wheels

1 lemon, cut into wheels

1 cup seeded and cubed honeydew melon

1 cup red grapes, halved

In a heavy medium saucepan over medium heat, combine the water, sugar, cloves, cinnamon, star anise, vanilla pod, and ginger. Bring to a boil, reduce to a simmer, and cook for 10 minutes. Turn off the heat and let sit for 30 minutes to infuse. Strain into a large bowl. Add the wine, juices, and fruits and stir well. Refrigerate overnight. Serve from pitchers over lots of ice.

SANGRIA BLANCA

White Sangria is something you really want in the summertime when nothing is going on and it's hot and very humid outside. We developed this recipe about six years ago and have loved it ever since. Highly suggested for afternoon gatherings and finger foods.   MAKES 2½ QUARTS

1 (750 ml) bottle Portuguese Vinho Verde

¾ cup simple syrup (page 154)

¾ cup Massenez crème de pêche

¼ cup freshly squeezed lemon juice

1 cup seeded and cubed cantaloupe

1 cup sliced peaches

1 cup green grapes, halved

1 cup red grapes, halved

Combine the wine, syrup, crème de pêche, and juice in a large bowl until well mixed. Add the fruits and refrigerate overnight. Serve from pitchers filled with lots of ice.

HOMEMADE SYRUPS, CORDIALS,

A T EMPLOYEES ONLY, we apply culinary techniques to our drink making and use homemade ingredients whenever appropriate—not because we hope to be viewed as chefs, but because we want to be the very best bartenders and mix the finest cocktails. Don't get us wrong—not all commercial products are bad. We use quality purées imported from France and syrups from Lebanon with flavors and textures that we could never re-create ourselves. We turn to homemade when we feel that quality is lacking or when we want deeper tastes or a special touch.

Freshly squeezed fruit juices and fresh fruit purées are the most basic of our homemade ingredients. We also craft our own syrups, cordials, infused vermouths, tonics, and bitters—these are the culmination of years of research in classic old bartending books, experimentation, and inspiration taken from our own backgrounds, as well as from the astounding array of foods that New York offers.

Most of the recipes in this chapter can be made with very little effort, yet they will elevate your cocktail making to new levels, and they attest to a genuine dedication to crafted cocktails. It is best to keep your creations refrigerated, when necessary, in food-safe containers. They can be distributed to plastic squeeze bottles to reduce mess and make handling easier and quicker.

INFUSIONS, AND ACCOMPANIMENTS

CITRUS JUICES

Adding freshly squeezed juices was our first baby step into the world of classic mixology. Many classically inspired cocktails rely on the intensity and high acidity of fresh citrus juices to stand up to 80-proof spirits. Juices help create body in the cocktail but must be balanced with a sweetener before the cocktail is complete. Whether you squeeze juice using a hand reamer or an electric juicer, you must strain it to remove the pulp. The pulp will bitterly taint the juice if it is allowed to sit in the mix too long. Juice should always be used fresh and kept refrigerated. It is important to label every batch of juice with the date when it was squeezed. Fresh juices lose their brightness after 24 hours.

SIMPLE SYRUP

Simple syrup is the most basic sweetener used in cocktails, and as the name states, it's simple—made of just sugar and water. Like salt, sugar is a flavor enhancer, and simple syrup is used to bring out the character of other cocktail ingredients. Its sweetness also balances acidic elements like citrus juices. Superfine sugar (also called bar sugar, a nod to its use by bartenders) is best for making simple syrup because the fine granules dissolve easily without heating.

There are two methods for making simple syrup: hot and cold. Most people are familiar with the hot method and do not realize that you can get the same result by simply stirring or shaking it. The cold method works only with superfine sugar. Standard granulated sugar requires heat to thoroughly dissolve all the granules. Either way, the sugar and water proportions are the same—one to one by volume; because there is a lot of air trapped between granules of sugar, we recommend measuring by weight. For those who don't own a kitchen scale, we offer a volume measurement as well.

MAKES 1 QUART

1½ pounds (3⅓ cups) superfine sugar
2 cups water

Hot Method: Combine the sugar and water in a large saucepan over medium heat. Bring to a boil, stirring continuously. Let the syrup cool, then store in a quart bottle.

Cold Method: Using a funnel, pour the sugar into a quart bottle. Add the water in small increments, capping and shaking between additions to loosen the sugar and free the trapped air. Once all the water has been added, continue to rotate the bottle until all the sugar is dissolved.

Store in the refrigerator. It will firm up when cold, so allow to return to room temperature before using. The syrup will keep for 4 days, refrigerated.

DEMERARA SIMPLE SYRUP

MAKES 1 QUART

1 pound demerara sugar
2 cups water

Combine the sugar and water in a saucepan over medium heat. Bring to a boil, then reduce the heat to low and simmer for 15 minutes. Let cool, then store in a bottle. The syrup will keep for 4 days, refrigerated.

HONEY SYRUP

When added straight from the bottle or jar, honey does not work well in chilled cocktails. It will stick to the sides of the shaker when the ice is introduced and will resist mixing. If you want the flavor of honey in cocktails, you must first dilute its texture, make it soluble, and make it into a syrup. Most honey syrups contain just honey and water, but we have added vanilla and orange peel to accentuate some of the key flavor notes in the honey. Acacia honey is light in flavor and fragrant and is one of the few honeys that is truly liquid and does not crystallize. This particular recipe was developed for our Mediterra cocktail (page 108), which was one of the most popular cocktails in the first years after Employees Only opened.

MAKES 1 QUART

3 cups water
1½ cups acacia honey
Peel of 1 orange, removed in large strips
1 whole vanilla bean, scored and scraped

Combine all the ingredients in a saucepan over medium heat, bring to a boil, and let simmer for 5 minutes. Let cool, then strain into a food-safe quart container for storing. Fill a labeled squeeze bottle for easiest use. The syrup will keep for 7 days, refrigerated.

SUBSTITUTING FOR SIMPLE SYRUP

Other natural sweeteners—raw sugar, honey, maple syrup, and agave nectar—can be turned into syrups for easy use in cocktails as an alternative to simple syrup. Be mindful when you swap in flavored syrup in a cocktail that requires simple syrup: any flavor added to a cocktail should contribute positively to the final flavor profile of the cocktail. For example, agave—from which tequila is made—will increase the depth of flavor in a Margarita; maple syrup would overpower it.

Making syrups takes a little trial and error. Start by slowly heating equal proportions of the sweetener and water in a saucepan. The consistency should be such that the flavor of the ingredient is prominent but the syrup still liquid enough to pour. For more elaborate syrups, try adding herbs, spices, or citrus peel to increase the depth of flavor. For example, honey syrup (left) is incredible with vanilla and orange zest.

FRESH PINEAPPLE SYRUP

Pineapple syrup is a very simple affair and a tasty sweetener made for use in the Pisco Punch (page 116). The flavor experience is different from using juice or fruit, because although it is clean, it picks up much of the vegetal characteristics of the pineapple. This syrup has many applications and can substitute for simple syrup to add more depth in tropical cocktails.

MAKES 1 QUART

2 cups fresh pineapple cubes
1 quart simple syrup (page 154)

Combine the fruit and syrup in a large food-safe container and refrigerate for 72 hours. Strain the syrup and discard the pineapple. Fill a labeled squeeze bottle for easiest use. The syrup will keep for 7 days, refrigerated.

MINT SYRUP

In many antiquated recipes for this Southern specialty, infusing mint syrup is a necessary step in making a proper Mint Julep (page 78). This is a very simple ingredient to make and will greatly enhance the flavor of the cocktails you use it in. It is traditionally used as an ingredient in juleps and smashes.

MAKES 1 QUART

About 50 fresh mint leaves
1 quart simple syrup (page 154)

Carefully and lightly bruise the mint leaves with a muddler or the back of a wooden spoon in a food-safe container. Pour the syrup over the leaves, cover, and refrigerate for 4 hours. Strain and keep refrigerated. Fill a labeled squeeze bottle for easiest use. The syrup will keep for about 3 days.

SPICY GINGER BEER

Ginger beer is often made as a live fermented brew, a time-consuming and messy process—our method shortcuts time, but not flavor. For a controlled version of premade ginger beer, use a soda siphon to provide carbonation.

MAKES ABOUT 4 QUARTS

2 pounds fresh gingerroot, peeled and coarsely chopped
1 English cucumber, unpeeled and coarsely chopped
2 fresh red chiles, chopped
1 cup fresh mint leaves
1 cup turbinado sugar
¾ cup acacia honey
2 cups water
¼ cup freshly squeezed lime juice
1 teaspoon black peppercorns
Chilled club soda, or water if using a soda siphon

Place the ginger and cucumber in a food processor and pulse until finely chopped. Pour them along with any juice into a large saucepan over medium heat and add the chilies, mint leaves, sugar, honey, water, juice, peppercorns, and soda. Bring to a boil and simmer for 15 minutes until the liquid becomes syrupy enough to coat the back of a spoon. Remove from the heat and let cool overnight. Strain the ginger beer through a fine-mesh sieve into a food-safe container and refrigerate; it will keep for 4 days, refrigerated.

The ratio of syrup to club soda is 1:3 when made to order. If using a soda siphon, pour 1 cup syrup and 3 cups water into a 1-liter soda siphon.

GRENADINE

Grenadine has suffered a tragic alteration at the hand of commercial producers, who have made it into an artificially flavored and colored, high-fructose corn syrup travesty that has nothing to do with the fruit for which it is named. (The word "grenadine" comes from the Spanish word for pomegranate, grenada.) Determined to revive the real deal, we crafted our own recipe using POM Wonderful pomegranate juice. We fortify it with Cardenal Mendoza aged Spanish brandy to help preserve it and add an additional depth of flavor. Alternatively, try our Employees Only brand (see the Resources section).

MAKES ABOUT 1 QUART

2½ cups pomegranate juice

1 cup simple syrup (page 154)

½ cup Cardenal Mendoza or other dark-rich brandy

Pour the pomegranate juice and syrup into a small saucepan and bring to a boil over medium heat. Decrease the heat to low and reduce the mixture until it becomes syrupy enough to coat the back of a spoon, about 20 minutes. Let cool and add the brandy. Pour into a food-safe container and store in the refrigerator until needed. Fill a labeled squeeze bottle for

easiest use. Grenadine will keep for 2 weeks, refrigerated.

LIME CORDIAL

Unfortunately, most lime cordials on the market today are some of the nastiest artificial garbage you could put into your body. With no strong-flavored natural options, many bartenders have been making their Gimlets (page 72) with fresh lime juice and simple syrup. Yet without the bitterness of the lime oils, a fresh Gimlet falls flat. We have created an alternative using lime juice and agave nectar and flavored with the oils of kaffir lime leaf. Kaffir lime leaves are traditionally used in Thai cooking and have a wonderful aroma. Lime leaves can be found in Asian markets and some specialty stores such as Whole Foods. You can also buy our Employees Only brand (see the Resources section).

MAKES ABOUT 1⅓ QUARTS

4 cups freshly squeezed lime juice

2½ cups raw light agave nectar

40 kaffir lime leaves, heavily bruised to release flavor

Place all the ingredients in a medium saucepan over medium heat. Bring to a boil, then decrease the heat to low. Simmer until the mixture becomes syrupy enough to coat the back of a spoon, about 35 minutes. Using a slotted spoon, scoop out all the leaves and any scum that may have risen to the surface. Strain through a fine-mesh sieve and store in a food-safe container. Keep refrigerated until use. Lime cordial will keep for 7 days, refrigerated. Fill a labeled squeeze bottle for easiest use.

WILD STRAWBERRY CORDIAL

Our wild strawberry cordial is actually somewhere between a fruit purée and a syrup. The idea was to create a high-octane strawberry flavor to blend in a French 75 cocktail (page 69). Much of the flavor comes from the wild strawberries we have imported frozen from France—they are tiny in size but big in flavor and vary from light yellow to deep red. You can use regular fresh strawberries, but make absolutely certain that they are ripe and fragrant.

MAKES ABOUT 1 QUART

4 pounds frozen or fresh strawberries, hulled
1 cup granulated sugar
1 cup water
Grated zest of ½ lemon
1 vanilla bean, scored and scraped

Place all the ingredients in a saucepan over medium heat. Bring to a boil, stirring, then decrease the heat to low and simmer for about 25 minutes. Remove from the heat and let cool. Strain out the lemon zest and vanilla bean and pour into a store-and-pour container. The cordial will keep for 7 days, refrigerated. Keep refrigerated until use. Fill a labeled squeeze bottle for easiest use.

HIBISCUS CORDIAL

Hibiscus is used throughout the Middle East and Latin America to make a ruby-red herbal tea. You can find the flowers at a tea or herb retailer. This hibiscus cordial is the brainchild of our bar manager and long-time friend Robert Krueger. This cleverly designed cordial brings out a rich color, beautiful floral notes, and a nice citrus flavor from the dried hibiscus flowers. It's the main ingredient in Rob's Roselle cocktail (page 71). Vodka and brandy serve to fortify the cordial for longer use.

MAKES ABOUT 1 QUART

2 cups water
½ cup dried hibiscus flowers
1½ pounds superfine sugar
2½ ounces 100-proof vodka
2½ ounces VS cognac

Bring the water to a boil in a medium saucepan over high heat. Decrease the heat and add the hibiscus flowers and sugar; stir until the sugar is entirely dissolved. Remove from the heat and allow to cool. Add the vodka and cognac, then strain and bottle immediately.

VERMOUTH DE PROVENCE

When first conceiving Employees Only, we knew we wanted to create our own house vermouths. We abandoned the idea of making our vermouth from raw wine and decided instead to use dry vermouth as a base for an infusion of additional herbs. The primary flavors in dry vermouth are rosemary, thyme, lavender, and anise—the same botanicals that make up the herbes de Provence blend used in cooking. To extract and transfuse flavors, we use a hot infusion method to create just a small amount of highly concentrated liquid that can be blended with the rest of a bottle of vermouth without cooking out all the alcohol. This controlled method of infusing reduces the amount of contact between alcohol and herbs—if left to steep too long, the finish is bitter. EO

Vermouth de Provence is one of the key ingredients in the Provençal cocktail (page 49).

MAKES 1 QUART

2 tablespoons herbes de Provence
1 (750 ml) bottle Noilly Prat dry vermouth

Place the herbes de Provence in a small saucepan over medium heat for 2 minutes, or until fragrant. Add 2 cups of the vermouth. Bring to a boil and immediately remove from the heat. Let stand until cool. Add the remaining vermouth and strain through cheesecloth. Bottle and store at room temperature. Will keep indefinitely.

CHAI-INFUSED SWEET VERMOUTH

Whereas dry vermouths are herbal, sweet vermouths are spice driven. When we decided to formulate our own sweet vermouth infusion with a deep, accentuated spiciness, we found the perfect warmth and fragrance in chai—the much-loved blend of black tea, cardamom, clove, cinnamon, and ginger. The resulting flavor is so sexy that you will feel like you have been kissed by a Bollywood beauty. This intoxicating concoction is the defining ingredient in our Mata Hari cocktail (page 102).

MAKES 1 QUART

4 green cardamom pods
4 whole cloves
1 cinnamon stick
1 tablespoon peeled, coarsely chopped gingerroot
1 tablespoon loose-leaf chai tea
1 (1-liter) bottle Cinzano sweet vermouth

Place the cardamom, cloves, cinnamon, and ginger in a small saucepan over low heat and heat until fragrant, about 2 minutes. Add the tea and 1 cup of the vermouth. Bring to a low boil for 2 minutes. Remove from the heat and let cool completely. Add the remaining vermouth and strain the mixture through cheesecloth. Bottle and store at room temperature. Will keep indefinitely.

RED BUSH–INFUSED VERMOUTH

This tea-infused vermouth was developed by EO bartender Milos Zica for the Quiet Storm cocktail (page 118). Also known as rooibos, South African red bush tea is a robust herbal tea with a rich mahogany color. We recommend the Silence rooibos tea blend from T Salon, which is where the cocktail's name partially derives from. Like the Vermouth de Provence (opposite), this vermouth is created with the hot infusion method that requires steeping the tea and other ingredients in a small amount of vermouth to make a concentrate. The color of this infused vermouth is a rich pumpkin orange.

MAKES ¾ QUART

1 (750 ml) bottle Dolin Blanc vermouth
1 tablespoon T Salon Silence red rooibos tea
Peel of 1 lemon, in strips

Pour 1 cup of the vermouth into a small saucepan over low heat. Add the tea and slowly bring to a boil, then remove immediately from the heat. Squeeze the lemon peel over the mixture, then drop it in. Stir gently and allow to cool for 30 minutes. Strain the infusion through cheesecloth into the vermouth bottle with the remaining vermouth. Store at room temperature. Will keep indefinitely.

LAVENDER-INFUSED GIN

Plymouth gin has a slightly floral nature. We accentuated it with dried lavender, creating a fast and versatile infusion with many possibilities. This infusion is visually stunning—the herb colors the gin with a slight hue of dark lavender. We use it as the base for our Provençal cocktail (page 49) and recommend it for making a lavender fizz or even an Aviation cocktail (page 63) made with lemon juice, maraschino liqueur, and infused gin.

MAKES 1 QUART

2 teaspoons organic dried lavender
1 (1-liter) bottle Plymouth gin

Place the lavender in a small saucepan over low heat. Add 2 cups of the gin and bring to a boil. Immediately remove from the heat and allow to cool. Add the remaining gin. Strain the mixture through cheesecloth into a bottle and discard the lavender. Store at room temperature away from sunlight. Will keep indefinitely.

PEACH-INFUSED BOURBON

Peaches and bourbon is about as Southern as you can get. Drying the fruit before steeping is key—the flavors are concentrated and yield a strong, clean peach essence; fresh fruit, on the other hand, releases its water into the liquid and dilutes the infusion. The only problem with dried peaches is that they will soak up some of the bourbon, resulting in some loss, but it is worth it. Today, high-quality dried peaches are available in most supermarkets, which greatly simplifies the process.

When the infused bourbon is tasted straight, the fruit flavor may seem subdued, but mixing it with sugar or sweetened ingredients awakens the peachiness. We created this infusion for our Pêche Bourbon cocktail (page 46).

MAKES ¾ QUART

12 dried organic unsulphured peach halves
1 (1-liter) bottle Maker's Mark bourbon

Place the peaches and bourbon in a large covered glass container or cookie jar. Let rest for 3 days, then strain into the bottle. Store at room temperature. Will keep indefinitely.

ENGLISH BISHOP

How to Mix Drinks or the Bon Vivant's Companion offers a recipe for English Bishop that involves sketchy directions and an open fire. It took some trial and error, but we adapted it to a standard oven. The infusion can be a cocktail sipped on its own, or an ingredient that can be mixed into other cocktails; we use it in our Jersey Devil cocktail (page 99).

MAKES ABOUT ¾ QUART

1 orange
30 whole cloves
1 (750 ml) bottle ruby port
1 cup superfine sugar

Preheat the oven to 400°F. Stud the orange with the cloves, place in a baking dish, and bake until the entire orange is browned, about 30 minutes. While still warm, carefully cut into quarters and place in a saucepan over medium heat. Add the port and simmer for 30 minutes. Remove the orange quarters, strain the liquid, and add the sugar. Allow to cool, strain out any debris, and bottle. Will keep for 2 weeks, refrigerated.

ABSINTHE BITTERS

Poring through old cocktail books, we noted that every reputable bar had a house recipe for bitters. Originally we played with infusing bitter herbs and spices in absinthe but found the task too time-consuming and the results too inconsistent. We settled instead on a blend of different absinthes, Green Chartreuse, and bitters to create just the right balance of anise and bitterness.

MAKES 1 QUART

3 cups Pernod 68 absinthe
½ cup Green Chartreuse
1 teaspoon Peychaud's bitters
1 teaspoon Angostura bitters
2 tablespoons Fee Brothers mint bitters

Combine all the ingredients in a liter bottle using a funnel. Cover or cork the bottle and gently turn it upside down three times to blend thoroughly. Store at room temperature. Will keep indefinitely.

BITTERS

Bitters do for a cocktail what pepper and bay leaves do for soup. Over the last few decades, bitters have not been a required ingredient in every cocktail; this does not mean they are reserved only for the cocktails of bygone eras. Bitters add depth, complexity, and a certain spark to cocktails. Once created for medicinal purposes, bitters are made by macerating bitter herbs and spices in high-proof spirits. They quickly found their way into cocktails, mainly to enhance the flavors of the rough rums and whiskeys of the past, making the spirits palatable in the form of a cocktail. Most bitters contain alcohol, and many of them are over 90 proof. In the old days of saloons and taverns, the barkeepers used to make their own bitters and guarded their recipes like gold. Today there are more styles of bitters on the market than ever, and bars are returning to the tradition of blending their own proprietary bitters.

EMPLOYEES ONLY CHICKEN SOUP

RECIPE BY CHEF JULIA JAKSIC

Every night around 4 a.m. at Employees Only, we offer up a hot cup of chunky chicken soup to the survivors of the long, cruel night. It is a tradition came by way of Greek night clubs. It is how we say "thank you" and "good night" to all the people who might expect one more drink.   MAKES 4½ TO 5 QUARTS

1 whole chicken, about 3½ pounds, rinsed

1 onion, cut into quarters

1 carrot, peeled and cut in half lengthwise

1 celery stalk, cut in half lengthwise

8 whole cloves garlic

2 bay leaves, preferably fresh

3 star anise

2 whole cloves

1 cinnamon stick

1 teaspoon red pepper flakes

1 teaspoon cardamom pods

3 tablespoons olive oil

1 small onion, diced

1 carrot, peeled and diced

2 celery stalks, diced

Salt and freshly ground black pepper

Place the chicken, onion, carrot, and celery in a large pot and pour in 3 quarts of water (the chicken should be completely submerged). Add the garlic, bay leaves, star anise, cinnamon, red pepper flakes, and cardamom. Bring to a boil over high heat, then decrease the heat and simmer, uncovered, for about 30 minutes, or until the chicken is cooked all the way through.

Remove the chicken from the pot and place it on a cutting board. Strain the broth through a fine-mesh strainer into a smaller pot and discard the solids. When the chicken is cool, remove the skin and cut the meat from the bones. Discard the skin and bones, cut the meat into bite-size pieces, and add them back to the broth. Bring the soup to a gentle simmer.

Meanwhile, in a sauté pan, heat the olive oil. Add the diced onion, carrot, and celery and sauté until tender, 6 to 10 minutes. Add the onion, carrot, and celery to the soup, season to taste with salt and pepper, and serve when drunk.

Afterword

IN THE WEE HOURS of December 27, 1930, five men sauntered into the West 45th Street speakeasy run by one Thomas Wassel and engaged him in earnest conversation, punctuating their speech with eight shots from the pistols they had hidden under their coats. He did not survive the conversation.

Fortunately, I've never seen anything like that happen at Employees Only. Indeed, it would have made me very sad if I had, as Jason and Dushan, its proprietors and the authors of the very fine book you're holding, are not only good friends of mine but also figures of no small importance in the modern Cocktail revolution. Employees Only was one of the very first bars dedicated to reviving the classic American art of the bar, and it remains one of the most successful. More than that, though, Dushan and Jason are bartenders to the last stir, and the world doesn't have nearly enough of those.

When I was first starting to loiter in groggeries, I did most of my drinking in old man's bars. They were cheap, and I was poor. But there was also something about the dignity of the gents behind the bar that made their joints far more congenial to me than the usual college bars, with their smutty drinks and bartenders who didn't know any more about life than I did. The old guys knew how to talk to every customer, and knew what to do in every odd situation that might arise.

Those are lessons that Jason and Dushan, working bartenders since before such creatures as "bar chefs," "celebrity mixologists," and "brand ambassadors" began to stalk the earth, managed to absorb. Even better, they've brought that old, bartenderly way to a new generation.

Finally, a word about this volume. *Speakeasy* is packed with good sense and intelligent advice, techniques are explained without condescension, and the recipes are carefully curated and contextualized and even fitted out with tasting notes. But for me all that isn't even the best part of this book. The authors very correctly note that "every cocktail should have an element that gives it zing and makes it special." The same is true with books, and I think in the case of Jason and Dushan the element that makes the difference is the same in both their cocktails and their writing: personality.

—David Wondrich

Resources

BAR TOOLS AND SUPPLIES

Uber Bar Tools
Best bar tools available.
www.uberbartools.com

Mister Mojito
Best muddlers on the market and some clever
bar tools too.
www.mistermojito.com

Cocktail Kingdom
Variety of eccentric bar tools and hard-to-find
bitters like the Bitter Truth.
www.cocktailkingdom.com

Minners Designs
Cool cocktail glassware.
www.minners.com

INGREDIENTS

Peychaud's Bitters and Regan's Orange Bitters
No. 6
Essential ingredients for a variety of classic
cocktails including the Sazerac and Dry Gin
Martini.
www.buffalotrace.com/giftshop.asp

Fee Brothers
Offers a variety of interesting bitters including
Old Fashion Bitters, Peach Bitters, Orange Bit-
ters, Mint Bitters, Lemon Bitters, Grapefruit
Bitters, Rhubarb Bitters, Cherry Bitters and
Whiskey Barrel Aged Bitters.
www.feebrothers.com

The Bitter Truth
Fantastic line of classically-inspired bitters from
an exceptionally talented German mixologist,
Stephan Berg. The choices include Aromatic
Bitters, Grapefruit Bitters, Orange Bitters, Jerry
Thomas Own Decanter Bitters, Lemon Bitters,
really delicious Celery Bitters and our favorite,
Chocolate "Xocolatl" Bitters. Also available is
a fantastic Orange Flower Water for a perfect
Ramos Gin Fizz.
http://the-bitter-truth.com

Boiron
Delicious line of French-made frozen fruit
purées with a minimal amount of sugar added
to boost flavors. Their White Peach Purée is
peerless as an ingredient for a Bellini.
www.boironfreres.com

Perfect Purée of Napa Valley
Great line of all-natural fruit purées made in the heart of Napa Valley.
www.perfectpuree.com

Employees Only Brands
Our little commercial venture that sells our all-natural, preservative-free Grenadine, Lime Cordial, and more.
www.employeesonlybrands.com

Cocktail Cherries
Luxardo maraschino cocktail cherries.
www.preissimports.com

OTHER USEFUL INFORMATION

The Museum of the American Cocktail
America's only museum devoted to preserve the history and evolution of the cocktail.
www.museumoftheamericancocktail.org

Ardent Spirits
Published by Gary Regan, this is a newsletter full of interesting information.
www.ardentspirits.com

Liquor.com
Phenomenal daily newsletter about all things on distilled spirits and their use.
www.liquor.com

Tales of the Cocktail
The world's biggest gathering of everything cocktail-related.
www.talesofthecocktail.com

King Cocktail
Dale DeGroff's website—full of recipes, advice, and resources.
www.kingcocktail.com

Thebarkeeper.com
A website dedicated to the on-premise drink industry.
www.thebarkeeper.com

Cocktail Data Base
Fantastic database with thousands of recipes.
www.cocktaildb.com

Employees Only
Stay in touch!
www.employeesonlynyc.com

Index